To Joan
Bon appetite
Ess mein Kinde
Love
Cevrit Murray

New Kosher Cooking

To Maxwell in memoriam.

New Kosher Cooking

Colette Rossant

Illustrated by James Rossant

ARBOR HOUSE

New York

Copyright © 1986 Footnote Productions Ltd.

Published in the United States of America by
Arbor House Publishing Company
and in Canada by
Fitzhenry & Whiteside, Ltd.

This book was designed and produced by
Footnote Productions Ltd.

Library of Congress Cataloging-in-Publication Data

Rossant, Colette.
  New kosher cooking.

  Includes index.
  1. Cookery, Jewish.   1. Title.
TX724.R584   1986   641.5′676   85-30663
ISBN 8-87795-802-5

Manufactured in the United States of America.

10 9 8 7 6 5 4 3 2 1

Contents

Introduction

A few years ago, a very good friend called to tell me her daughter was getting married and to ask for my help with the wedding reception. When I asked the traditional question, "Who is the lucky young man?" there was a pause at the other end of the line. Finally my friend said, "Philip is a wonderful young man but . . . he is an orthodox Jew. In fact, my daughter will be keeping a kosher home. Colette, I am glad my daughter is making a commitment to her religion, but I wanted the food at her wedding to be something special and now it will have to be so ordinary!" My response to that was, "Certainly the food can be special. We'll just think of it as a challenge." With that, we set to work to develop interesting new recipes for the wedding—recipes that happened to be kosher as well.

The wedding day finally came. After the traditional ceremony, drinks were served, accompanied by cherry tomatoes filled with my own version of chopped chicken liver and mushrooms stuffed with baked salmon and capers. At that point, though, there was too much excitement for anyone to notice the food. Then we all sat down to dinner. Some eyebrows were raised when the appetizer arrived: stuffed smoked salmon with asparagus purée, followed by veal pâté on a bed of endive. When the main course came along, stuffed shoulder of lamb with Japanese shiso leaves, served with a julienne of young vegetables and fresh noodles in a mushroom sauce, I heard some murmurs. But as the meal was being cleared away, the father of the bridegroom raised his glass for a toast to the cook, and everyone joined him with enthusiasm. I had succeeded! The wedding dinner was a superb and strictly kosher meal. By the time dessert came, dozens of wedding guests had approached me to ask for recipes. That was when I decided to write this book.

A tremendous religious revival is taking place across the United States today. Many young Jews are tracing their roots and yearning for family, tradition, and a sense of belonging, but with an added sophistication. These newly observant people know what good food is; they are *au courant* when it comes to eating. Their knowledge of wine is impressive, their taste in food refined, yet they have an unwavering determination to respect Jewish dietary laws.

Many of the recent developments in the "new" cuisine are accessible to those who keep kosher. Lighter foods and shorter cooking times make for better food, whether kosher or not. Further, our food has become so international in scope and influence that scores of new and different spices, seasonings, fruits, vegetables, and other foods are all readily available. With a little imagination, these new ingredients can add interest, variety, and subtlety to kosher cooking, all within the limitations of the dietary laws.

In my efforts to bring the elements of the new cuisine to kosher cooking, I've had some failures—sometimes the traditional recipes are the best recipes. But often a small change turns an old recipe into something new. For example, traditional matzoh balls become completely different when a pea-sized bit of beef marrow is placed in the center of each one. Ordinary pot roast becomes special when fresh cranberries are added.

Kosher cooking has always been full of ingenious ways to observe the dietary laws and create the *illusion* of breaking them—nondairy creamers are a good example. Today's kosher cook can do far better than that. For example, I like to substitute silken bean curd (several kosher brands are available) for heavy cream in French-style meat dishes; creamy-tasting desserts can be made using agar-agar, a natural gelatin made from seaweed.

Keeping a kosher kitchen is a little more complicated than keeping any good kitchen, but the rules are easily mastered. Since a number of excellent kosher cookbooks explain the details, I won't discuss them here. Remember, however, that any rabbi will be happy to explain the dietary laws.

To use this cookbook successfully, use it with an open mind. Although these recipes are not traditional, they are kosher. Some recipes call for unusual ingredients, but they can easily be found in well-stocked food stores and in most Oriental groceries. (A glossary at the back of the book explains these ingredients in detail.) It helps to have a love of good food, a sense of humor, and a spirit of adventure. Bon appetit.

Appetizers

Spreads, Pâtés and Terrines

Tajine Menina
𝄞 (Algerian Chicken 𝄞 Pâté)

Serves 6

*T*his was one of my favorite dishes when I went to visit my Aunt Nadia, who lived in Algeria. She would serve this soft chicken pâté, molded with hard-boiled eggs in the center, with a spicy tomato sauce. I like it with Green Sauce (see page 242) or Ginger Sauce (see page 239). Serve it accompanied by sautéed string beans.

2 quarts water
1 fresh mint sprig or
⅛ teaspoon dried mint
1 fresh thyme sprig or
⅛ teaspoon dried thyme
2 onions
2 cloves
1 leek
3 pounds chicken pieces
1 celery stalk
1 orange zest, julienned

salt
freshly ground black pepper
8 slices white bread
½ cup Chicken Stock (see
page 49)
1 hot green pimento
3 eggs, separated
1 tablespoon margarine
3 hard-boiled eggs
parsley sprigs, for garnish

In a large pot, bring the water to a boil with the mint and the thyme. Quarter 1 onion and add it to the soup. Stick the remaining onion with the 2 cloves and add it to the soup.

Wash the leek, cut it into 3 pieces and add to the soup. Add the chicken, celery, orange zest, salt and black pepper to taste. Lower the heat to medium and cook, uncovered, for 1 hour. Remove from the heat; remove the chicken onto a plate to cool.

In a large bowl, soak the bread in the Chicken Stock.

Remove and discard the chicken skin. Remove all the meat from the bones and coarsely chop it. Discard the bones. Place the meat in a large mixing bowl.

Preheat the oven to 425°F.

Squeeze the liquid from the bread. Place the bread, 4 tablespoons of the chicken, and the hot pimento in a food processor and process until all the ingredients are finely chopped. Add to the coarsely chopped chicken. Add the egg yolks and salt and black pepper to taste. Mix well.

In a large bowl, beat the egg whites with a pinch of salt until they hold a peak. Fold the egg whites into the chicken mixture.

Grease a 2-quart pâté dish with the margarine.

Fill the bottom of the dish with half the chicken mixture. Place the hard-boiled eggs in the center and cover them with the remaining chicken mixture.

Bake for 10 minutes. Cover the dish with aluminum foil, reduce the temperature to 350°F and bake for 30 minutes longer.

Remove the pâté from the oven. Pass the blade of a knife around the edges. Slice the pâté in the dish. Garnish the dish with parsley sprigs and serve tepid.

Pot Roast Pâté with ❧ Cranberries and ❧ Avocado Sauce

Serves 10

*A*gar-agar is natural seaweed which can be used to replace unflavored packaged gelatine. It can be found in any health food store.

1 cooked Pot Roast (see page 124)
3 sticks agar-agar or 4 envelopes kosher unflavored gelatine
4 cups Chicken Stock (see page 49)
12 black olives, pitted and halved lengthwise
1 carrot, scraped and thinly sliced
2 bunches watercress

1 cup cooked, drained cranberries
salt
black pepper
1 avocado, pitted and peeled
1 garlic clove, peeled
3 tablespoons lemon juice
2 tablespoons vegetable oil
1 teaspoon ground cumin
parsley sprigs, for garnish
lime slices, for garnish

Slice the pot roast as thin as possible. Set aside.

Soak the agar-agar in enough cold water to cover for 15 minutes. Squeeze the water out and cut the agar-agar into small pieces. In a small saucepan, melt the agar-agar in ½ cup of the Chicken Stock over low heat. Add the melted agar-agar to the remaining stock and set aside.

In a large earthenware terrine or other mold, arrange the olives, skin-side down, alternately with the sliced carrots. Pour 1 cup of the agar-agar mixture over them and refrigerate.

Wash the watercress and pat dry with paper towels.

Discard the tough stems and finely chop the leaves.

When the first layer of agar-agar has nearly set but is still slightly soft to the touch, cover it with slices of pot roast, overlapping the edges. Sprinkle some watercress and cranberries over the slices, then make another layer of meat and sprinkle it with the remaining watercress and cranberries. Slowly pour the remaining agar-agar over the meat, filling the terrine. Cover with aluminum foil and refrigerate for 2 hours or overnight.

To make the sauce, in a food processor place the avocado, garlic, lemon juice, oil and cumin. Process until the ingredients are puréed. Pour the purée into a bowl, add salt and black pepper to taste, mix well and refrigerate until ready to serve.

To serve, unmold the pâté onto a round platter. Garnish with parsley sprigs and lime slices.

Serve with the avocado sauce.

❧ Japanese-Style ❧ Terrine of Sole

Serves 6

*S*ansho pepper is not really pepper but a rather brown, tangy Japanese spice made from the berries of the sansho plant. It is available in Oriental food stores, and will keep indefinitely stored in an airtight container in a cool, dry place. It can be replaced by very finely chopped lemon peel, available in all supermarkets. Serve this terrine with Summer Tomato Salad (see page 70).

8 cups Fish Stock (see
    page 48)
½ cup sake
3 shallots, peeled
12 sole fillets, about
    3 pounds
2 sticks agar-agar or
    3 envelopes kosher
    unflavored gelatine
1 tablespoon light soy sauce
¼ teaspoon saffron
salt

freshly ground black pepper
¼ tablespoon vegetable oil
sansho pepper
6 small zucchinis, about
    4 inches long, thinly
    sliced
1 cup pitted black olives,
    coarsely chopped
2 tablespoons chopped
    chives
parsley sprigs, for garnish
2 lemons, cut into wedges

In a large, deep skillet, place the Fish Stock, sake and shallots. Bring to a boil, lower the heat and simmer for 10 minutes. Add the sole fillets, reduce the heat to low and cook for 4 minutes. Remove the fillets with a spatula and put them on a platter to cool.

Tear the agar-agar sticks into several pieces. Place them in a large bowl, add enough cold water to cover and soak for 10 minutes.

Strain the fish stock through a very fine sieve placed over a large bowl. Measure out 6 cups of the stock and pour it into a saucepan.

Squeeze the water out of the agar-agar pieces and add them to the fish stock. Add the light soy sauce, saffron and salt and black pepper to taste. Bring to a boil, lower the heat to medium and cook for 5 minutes, stirring constantly, until all the agar-agar has melted.

Oil a 2-quart pâté mold with the vegetable oil.

Fill the pâté mold to a depth of 1 inch with the fish jelly. Refrigerate for 10 minutes, or until the jelly is set. Top the jelly with a layer of sole; sprinkle the fish with salt, black pepper and sansho pepper to taste. Cover the fish with a layer of sliced zucchini. Sprinkle the zucchini with some of the chopped olives and chopped chives. Pour enough fish jelly over the zucchini to cover it (about ½ cup) and refrigerate for 10 minutes or until the jelly has set.

Repeat the above steps until all the fish, zucchini, olives and chives are used. Pour the remaining jelly over the last layer and refrigerate, covered, overnight.

To unmold the terrine, run a knife around the edges of the mold, then place an oval platter upside down over the mold. Invert the mold and platter together and the terrine should slide out easily.

Garnish the platter with the parsley sprigs and serve with lemon wedges.

❦ Terrine of Salmon ❦

Serves 6

*T*his is a very simple and elegant recipe to serve for dinner on a hot summer night with a fresh green salad, crisp French bread, a strawberry tart and iced dry white wine.

1 teaspoon vegetable oil
2 pounds whiting fillets, cut into 2-inch pieces
3 egg whites
4 cakes silken bean curd
1 tablespoon brandy
salt
freshly ground black pepper
4 pounds thin salmon fillets
2 tablespoons chopped fresh mint or ¾ tablespoon dried mint

1 tablespoon grated ginger or 1 teaspoon dried ground ginger
1 teaspoon drained small capers
½ teaspoon lime juice
8 fresh mint leaves
2 thin carrot slices
1 Japanese cucumber, thinly sliced.

Preheat the oven to 375°F. Oil a 1½-quart baking dish, 4 inches deep, with the vegetable oil.

In a food processor combine the whiting, egg whites, brandy and 2 of the bean curd cakes. Process until the ingredients are puréed. Pour the purée into a bowl, add salt and black pepper to taste and mix well.

Spread a layer of the purée in the baking dish. Cover with a layer of salmon fillets and sprinkle with salt and black pepper. Repeat the above step to make additional layers, finishing with a layer of whiting.

Place the baking dish in a larger deep baking dish. Fill the larger dish with enough water to come three-quarters of the way up the sides of the smaller dish.

Bake the terrine for 1 hour. Remove the dish from the oven and cool at room temperature. Cover and refrigerate until well chilled.

To make the sauce, drain the remaining bean curd well. In a medium bowl, beat the bean curd with a whisk until smooth. Add the chopped mint, grated ginger, capers, lime juice and salt and black pepper to taste. Pour the sauce into a sauceboat and refrigerate until ready to serve.

To unmold the terrine, run a knife around the edges of the mold, then place an oval platter upside down over the mold. Invert mold and platter together, and the terrine should slide out easily. Garnish the top by arranging mint leaves like the petals of two flowers and placing a carrot slice in the center of each flower. Surround the terrine with overlapping Japanese cucumber slices.

Serve with the sauce on the side.

🍆 Tapenade 🍆

Serves 6

*M*y mother lived in Provence in an old mas, *a Provençal farm house. Her housekeeper made the most wonderful tapenade—a mixture of black olives and anchovies—which she served on very thin toast around 5 o'clock in the afternoon with a cool* pastis, *the French anise drink. This is an adaptation of her recipe.*

20 black Greek olives, pitted
4 anchovies packed in olive oil, drained
2 garlic cloves, peeled
2 tablespoons drained capers
¼ teaspoon powdered bay leaf
¼ teaspoon dried thyme
freshly ground black pepper
½ cup olive oil
1½ tablespoons lemon juice
18 thin slices French bread
3 tablespoons grated daikon or Crème Fraîche (see page 231)
2 tablespoons chopped parsley

In a food processor, place the garlic, anchovies, capers, olives, bay leaf powder, thyme and freshly ground black pepper to taste. Process until all the ingredients are thinly chopped. Remove to a bowl. Add the olive oil and lemon juice. Mix well.

Toast the bread slices until they are lightly browned on both sides.

Spread some tapenade on the toast. Place some grated daikon or Crème Fraîche in the center and sprinkle with chopped parsley.

The remaining tapenade can be stored in a tightly sealed jar and refrigerated for several weeks.

Terrine of Turkey with Calvados

Serves 8

My stepfather loved Calvados, the apple brandy of Normandy. When I married and moved to the United States, every year he would send an eau-de-Cologne bottle filled with his best Calvados. One year he came to visit us. I made him a terrine of turkey breast with applejack, American apple brandy. He declared the terrine superb because, he said, he had detected the faint taste of his Calvados in it.

1 head celery
3 tablespoons olive oil
1 boneless turkey breast, cut into halves
4 carrots, diced
½ pound pearl onions, halved if large
3 tablespoons sugar
¼ cup Calvados or applejack
salt
freshly ground black pepper

5 envelopes kosher unflavored gelatine or 4 sticks agar-agar (see page 00)
1½ quarts apple juice
1 box frozen small green peas (petits pois), defrosted
1 sprig rosemary, for garnish
1 head Boston lettuce
1 cup Sweet Red Pepper Sauce (see page 235)

Remove the large green celery stalks and set them aside for another use. Dice the remaining yellow, tender celery stalks and leaves. Set aside.

In a large skillet, heat the oil over high heat. Add the turkey and brown on both sides. Then add the celery, carrots and pearl onions. Sauté for 3 to 4 minutes over high heat, then reduce the heat and simmer for 10 minutes. Sprinkle the turkey and vegetables with the sugar and raise the heat. Cook until the ingredients are caramelized, about 2 to 3 minutes. Pour the Calvados or applejack into the skillet and carefully ignite it with a match. When the flames die, reduce the heat and simmer, covered, for 10 minutes longer. Remove from the heat and let cool.

If using kosher unflavored gelatine, place the gelatine in a bowl. Add enough cold water to make a thin paste. If using agar-agar for the next step, soak the agar-agar in enough cold water to cover for 5 minutes. Drain and squeeze the water out. Tear in several pieces.

Heat the apple juice in a saucepan. Add the agar-agar or gelatine and stir with a wooden spoon over low heat until it is all dissolved (agar-agar will dissolve more quickly). If using gelatine, remove the saucepan from the heat and cool at room temperature for 1 hour before proceeding to the next step; if using agar-agar, turn off the heat but keep the liquid warm.

Pour a layer of gelatine or agar-agar 1 inch deep into a porcelain terrine. If using gelatine, refrigerate for 30 minutes; if using agar-agar, let it set at room temperature.

Remove the turkey from the skillet and dice.

Mix the peas with the vegetables in the skillet. Add salt and black pepper to taste.

Place some pieces of turkey and some vegetables on top of the gelatine or agar-agar layer. Do not cover the layer entirely; when the terrine is sliced, the pieces of turkey and vegetable should be surrounded by jelly. Sprinkle some of the cooking liquid from the skillet over the layer.

Repeat this layering procedure until all the turkey and vegetables are used up. End with a layer of agar-agar or gelatine. Garnish the top with rosemary leaves, cover with aluminum foil and refrigerate overnight.

To serve, line an oval serving platter with lettuce leaves. Heat the blade of a knife under hot water and pass it around the edges of the terrine. Unmold the terrine onto another platter and slice it. Arrange the slices on the lettuce and serve with Red Pepper Sauce.

Chopped Chicken Livers

Serves 6

One of my daughter's college roommates was Niamani, a lovely young woman from Kenya. We had her as a guest for a long weekend. One night she made us some chicken livers Kenya-style. Serve this unusual and delicious dish with toasted thin bagel slices or crackers.

2 tablespoons goose, duck or chicken fat
1 large onion, chopped
½ pound fresh chicken livers
4 hard-boiled eggs
1 teaspoon Dijon mustard

1 teaspoon anchovy paste
1 teaspoon dried tarragon
⅛ teaspoon cayenne
salt
¼ cup chopped toasted almonds

In a skillet, melt the fat over medium-high heat. When the fat is hot, add the onion, reduce the heat to medium and sauté until light brown.

Add the chicken livers and sauté until the livers are firm but still light pink inside. Place the livers and onions in a food processor and process until finely chopped but not puréed. Remove to a mixing bowl.

Put the eggs in the processor and chop them finely.

Add the mustard, anchovy paste, tarragon, cayenne and salt to the chicken livers. Mix well; add the chopped eggs. Mix again and correct the seasonings.

Arrange the chopped chicken livers in a glass serving bowl. Sprinkle the top with the chopped almonds.

❦ Baked Salmon Rillettes ❦

Serves 6 to 8

Rillettes is a French dish of meat slowly cooked in goose or other fat, then mashed with spices. It is usually served cold as an appetizer with bread. Every housewife in France has her own recipe for rillettes. One day I experimented with some firm baked salmon and found it made delicious rillettes. Use it to fill miniature puff pastry shells as an appetizer. Or simply put the rillettes in a bowl and serve with slices of fresh black or rye bread.

1 pound baked salmon
6 tablespoons unsalted
    butter, at room
    temperature
zest of 2 limes, grated
freshly ground black pepper
salt
2 tablespoons drained
    capers

1 tablespoon chopped
    mixed fresh herbs in
    season
24 miniature puff pastry
    shells
1½ cups mustard sprouts or
    alfalfa sprouts
1 Bermuda onion, thinly
    sliced
2 sour pickles, thinly sliced

Remove any bones and skin from the salmon. Cut the salmon into 2-inch cubes and put them in a bowl. With two forks, flake the fish well.

In another bowl, mash the butter with the lime zest. Add the softened butter to the salmon and mix well with a fork. Add black pepper and salt to taste and the capers and herbs. Mix again.

Put the rillettes into a serving bowl. Decorate the top with the mustard sprouts or alfalfa sprouts. Place 2 overlapping onion slices and 3 sour pickle slices on each individual serving plate.

Stuffed Appetizers

❧ Stuffed Smoked ❧ Salmon

Serves 6

A few years ago, while traveling in Japan, I stayed with the family of a New York friend. Most of the time, Japanese families invite you out to dinner, but Mrs. Futagawa was a superb cook, and she cooked for us. One night she served stuffed salmon. The dish looked superb. Thin slices of smoked salmon were stuffed with something green—stalks of thin asparagus. She said it was easy to make and promised to give me the recipe. Back in America, I tried it and found that this very elegant appetizer requires patience to make but is really worth the effort.

5 tablespoons olive oil
3 tablespoons lemon juice
freshly ground black
   pepper
1 pound smoked salmon,
   thinly sliced
4 tablespoons chopped
   parsley
4 tablespoons chopped basil
4 tablespoons chopped
   chervil
salt

1 package toasted nori
   (dried seaweed)
1 pound thin asparagus,
   cooked until crisp
1 cup Crème Fraîche (see
   page 231) or sour cream
2 tablespoons drained
   capers
2 tablespoons drained pink
   peppercorns
mint leaves, for garnish
1 lemon, sliced, for garnish

Cut 2 pieces of waxed paper into rectangles about 10 inches wide and 14 inches long.

In a small bowl, mix together 3 tablespoons of the olive oil with 2 tablespoons of the lemon juice. Add black pepper to taste and mix well. Brush the waxed paper with the mixture.

Arrange the smoked salmon slices on the waxed paper, overlapping each slice by ¼ inch.

Combine the parsley, basil and chervil in a bowl. Add 1 tablespoon olive oil and black pepper to taste. If the salmon is not salty, sprinkle it with salt to taste. Spread the mixture evenly over the salmon slices. Cover the herbs with a layer of toasted nori sheets.

Trim the white parts from the asparagus. Arrange the asparagus in a line down the center of the salmon.

Roll up the salmon slices on the wider side of the waxed paper. Holding the edges of the paper, roll it up about 1 inch; press the salmon down and carefully detach the waxed paper. Continue rolling the salmon, always detaching the waxed paper. When the salmon is rolled, carefully wrap it in a fresh piece of waxed paper and refrigerate overnight.

In a bowl, mix the Crème Fraîche with 1 tablespoon of the lemon juice and add the capers. To serve, use a very sharp knife to cut the salmon rolls into ½-inch slices, then carefully remove the waxed paper. Arrange several slices on each individual serving plate. Garnish with a few pink peppercorns. Place 1 tablespoon of crème frâiche in the center of each plate. Garnish with 2 mint leaves and a slice of lemon.

🍂 Meat Sausages 🍂
en Croûte

Serves 4 to 6

*T*he best use for leftover pot roast I know was first served to me by my mother's old friend Irene. A diminutive lady of about 60 when I first met her, Irene was a "Haute Couture Modiste"—she made hats for fashion designers. She made my wedding crown, a magnificent circle of hand-made violets. When I went to try it on, she served me delicious little cakes of light pastry filled with meat. I kept eating them as my mother scolded me, saying I would never fit into my wedding dress. But who could resist the temptation!

Later, when I went to say goodbye before leaving for the States, Irene handed me her recipe. Since then, her recipe has become a staple in our family. My married daughter makes them for her guests, my son asks for them every time he is home from college and my husband complains he is putting on weight—but he asks why I don't make them more often. These meat-filled pastry sticks can be frozen, and then baked without defrosting whenever unexpected guests come for dinner.

Dough:

1¾ cups all-purpose flour

1 stick margarine plus
    1 tablespoon for baking
    pan

¼ teaspoon salt

1 egg

¼ cup ice water

2 tablespoons vegetable oil

flour for rolling

Filling:

1 tablespoon vegetable oil	1 tablespoon tarragon
1 onion, chopped	3 tablespoons gravy from
2 garlic cloves, chopped	the Pot Roast
2 tablespoons pine nuts	2 eggs
3 cups cooked Pot Roast,	salt
chopped (see page 124)	freshly ground black pepper
1 egg, beaten	parsley sprigs, for garnish

To make the dough, place the flour, margarine and salt in a food processor. Process until the mixture forms a coarse meal.

In a bowl with a pouring lip, mix together the egg, ice water and oil. With the motor running, slowly add the ice-water mixture to the flour until the dough forms a ball. Wrap the dough in waxed paper and refrigerate until ready to use.

To make the filling, heat the oil in a skillet over high heat. Add the onion, reduce the heat to medium and sauté until transparent. Add the garlic and the pine nuts and cook until the garlic is light brown. Remove from the heat.

In a large bowl, combine the Pot Roast, onion mixture, tarragon and 2 eggs. Mix well, add the gravy and mix again. Add salt and black pepper to taste. Set aside.

Preheat the oven to 350°F.

Cut the dough in half; cut each half into thirds. On a floured board, roll a piece of the dough into a rectangle about 15 inches long and 4 inches wide. Arrange some of the meat mixture in a line down the center of the dough. Roll up the dough, enclosing the meat, so that it looks like a long, thin sausage. Moisten the edges of the dough with water and press them together. Place the roll in a buttered baking dish. Repeat with the remaining dough and meat mixture. At this point the rolls can be wrapped in waxed paper and frozen.

Brush the rolls with the beaten egg and bake for 25 minutes or until golden brown. Cut each stick into 2-inch pieces and serve garnished with parsley sprigs.

Mushroom Caps Stuffed with Salmon

Serves 6

12 large mushrooms
5 tablespoons unsalted
  butter
½ pound fresh salmon
¼ pound smoked salmon,
  thinly sliced

1½ tablespoons lemon juice
freshly ground black pepper
salt, if desired
1 head Boston lettuce
1 tablespoon chopped
  parsley

Wash the mushrooms, remove the stems (set them aside for another use) and pat the mushroom caps dry with paper towels. Set aside.

In a medium skillet, melt 2 tablespoons of the butter over medium-high heat. Add the fresh salmon and cook for 3 minutes on one side; turn and cook for another 3 minutes. Remove to a plate.

In the same skillet, sauté the smoked salmon for 1 minute on each side. Remove to the plate with the fresh salmon and add the lemon juice. With a fork, mash both salmons together to make a coarse purée.

In a small saucepan, melt the remaining butter. Add the melted butter to the mashed salmon, adding black pepper to taste and some salt if desired.

Fill the mushroom caps with the salmon mixture. Sprinkle each cap with some chopped parsley. Line each individual serving plate with lettuce leaves. Place the mushrooms on the leaves and serve.

ই Cheese Filo ই

Serves 6

*F*ilo *(also spelled phyllo) is a very thin dough that is often used for Middle Eastern and Oriental pastries, as well as for strudel. It comes in rolled sheets in a box and is available in most food stores. Remove what you need from the box and freeze the remaining dough. It will keep several weeks.*

1 pound farmer cheese	1 tablespoon drained capers
¼ pound feta cheese	1 tablespoon baking powder
2 tablespoons chopped black Greek olives	3 sheets filo dough
2 tablespoons chopped parsley	4 tablespoons melted unsalted butter
	2 eggs, beaten

In a large bowl, combine the farmer cheese with the feta cheese, olives, parsley, capers and baking powder. Mix well and set aside.

Cut the filo dough into long strips 2 inches wide.

Place one strip on the worktable and brush with butter. Place another strip of filo on top and brush again with butter. Continue this step 4 more times, stacking the strips.

Place a tablespoon of the cheese mixture at one end of a strip and fold the dough in a triangle (see illustration). Set aside. Repeat until all the cheese mixture is used; there should be about 12 to 15 triangles.

Preheat the oven to 375°F.

Butter a baking sheet and arrange the triangles of dough side by side on it, leaving some space around each triangle. Brush each triangle with beaten egg.

Bake until golden brown, about 6 to 8 minutes. Serve hot.

❦ Veal Wonton ❦

Serves 4

*W*onton wrappers are small, thin squares of dough that are available packaged or fresh in most Oriental grocery stores. However, it is not very difficult to make your own using the recipe below. If you make a large batch, freeze half and use half for this recipe. Serve these wonton with sautéed long string beans.

¾ pound chopped lean veal
4 water chestnuts, finely chopped
2 scallions, trimmed and chopped
2 tablespoons sake or dry white wine
1½ tablespoons dark soy sauce
1½ teaspoons sesame oil
1 teaspoon finely chopped lemon peel

2 garlic cloves, finely chopped
salt
freshly ground black pepper
20 Wonton Wrappers (see below)
vegetable oil for frying
2 garlic cloves, thinly sliced
2 teaspoons finely chopped fresh ginger
watercress sprigs, for garnish

In a mixing bowl, combine the veal and the water chestnuts, scallions, sake, soy sauce, sesame oil, lemon peel, garlic, and salt and black pepper to taste. Mix well.

Place about a teaspoon of the mixture in the center of each wonton skin. Wet the edges of the wonton skins. Fold two opposite corners together to form a triangle; then press the edges together to enclose the filling. Join the two points at the base of the triangle and press them together (see illustration). Set the wonton aside.

In a saucepan, bring 1 quart of water to a boil. Add the wontons and cook for 2 minutes. Remove the saucepan from the heat and drain the wontons well.

Fill a medium skillet with oil to a depth of ½ inch. Heat the oil until hot; add the sliced garlic and the ginger. Cook, stirring constantly, for 1 minute. Add the cooked wonton and cook, stirring, until the wontons are golden brown. Remove to a platter, using a slotted spoon, and garnish with watercress sprigs.

❦ Wonton Wrappers ❦

Makes 24 wrappers

2 cups sifted all-purpose
   flour
1 teaspoon salt

1 egg, lightly beaten
½ cup cold water

In a food processor, mix together the flour and the salt. While the machine is running, add the eggs and then the water. Stop the machine as soon as the water is mixed into the flour. Remove the dough to a floured board and gather it into a ball. Knead the dough for 2 minutes, or until it is smooth but still soft.

Divide the dough into 4 equal balls. Roll out each ball into sheets ¹⁄₁₆ inch thick. With a dough cutter or sharp knife, cut each sheet into six 3½-inch squares.

If using the wrappers right away, dust them with flour and stack them.

To freeze the wrappers, stack them between squares of waxed paper. Frozen wrappers should be defrosted overnight in the refrigerator before using.

❦ Crêpes ❦

Makes 16 crêpes

*C*rêpes can be made several days in advance and refrigerated until ready to use. However, if the crêpes are going to be refrigerated for more than a couple of hours, barely cook the second side. To reheat, butter a crêpe pan and cook the second side for 1 minute. If you are making the crêpes for dessert, add the sugar.

3 large eggs
½ cup heavy cream
½ cup milk
6 tablespoons all-purpose
   flour
4 tablespoons melted
   unsalted butter

⅛ teaspoon salt
2 tablespoons sugar
   (optional)
1 tablespoon unsalted butter

In a blender or a food processor, place the eggs, cream, milk, flour, melted butter, salt—and sugar if used. Process until the ingredients are well mixed and the batter is smooth.

Pour the batter into a bowl and let it stand for 1 hour at room temperature.

Melt ½ teaspoon butter in a crêpe pan over medium-high heat. When the butter bubbles, pour 3 tablespoons of batter into the pan. Quickly tilt and rotate the pan until the batter coats its surface.

When the edges of the crêpe are lightly browned, turn it over with a spatula and cook for 1 to 2 minutes longer. Slide the crêpe onto a plate. Place a square of waxed paper on top.

Without adding more butter, pour 3 more tablespoons of batter into the pan and make another crêpe. Stack it on top of the first. Continue making crêpes, adding ½ teaspoon butter as needed, until all the batter is used.

Crêpes Stuffed with
❦ Smoked Salmon and ❦
Artichoke Hearts

Serves 4

6 ounces smoked salmon, chopped

2 tablespoons chopped fresh basil or ¾ teaspoon dried basil

2 4-ounce jars marinated Italian artichoke hearts, drained

1 pound farmer cheese

freshly ground black pepper

16 Crêpes (see page 30)

2 cups Hollandaise Sauce (see page 240)

5 tablespoons grated Swiss cheese

2 tablespoons unsalted butter

parsley sprigs, for garnish

Preheat the oven to 375°F.

In a mixing bowl, combine the salmon and basil.

Coarsely chop the artichokes. Add them to the salmon mixture. Add the farmer cheese, sprinkle with black pepper and mix well.

Spread some of the filling down the center of each Crêpe. Roll up the crêpes. Use a little of the butter to grease a baking dish and place the crêpes in the dish, seam-side-down. Bake for 10 minutes.

Remove the dish from the oven. Turn on the broiler. Pour the Hollandaise sauce over the crêpes, sprinkle the top with the Swiss cheese and dot with the remaining butter. Broil for 2 to 3 minutes or until the top is golden brown. Garnish with parsley sprigs and serve immediately.

❧ Tarragon Blini ❧

Serves 8

When I was 17 years old, I caught pneumonia and was very ill for several weeks. To help me recuperate, my parents sent me to the mountains to stay with a Russian family, the Pushrarovs, who would see to it that I got plenty of rest and ate well. This is where I discovered blini! We had them every Sunday, a dozen of them for each of us, while listening to old Caruso records. This recipe was given to me by Boris, Mrs. Pushrarov's younger son.

5½ cups milk	1 tablespoon dried tarragon
2½ teaspoons active dry yeast	½ teaspoon sugar
1¼ cups all-purpose flour	¼ teaspoon cayenne pepper
4 eggs, separated	salt
	vegetable oil for cooking

Heat the milk in a saucepan until it is hot, but do not let it boil. Place 4 cups of the milk in a bowl and add the yeast. Stir well. Measure 6 tablespoons of the flour into another large bowl. Pour in the milk and yeast mixture, stirring constantly. Place the batter in a warm place and let it ferment for 2 hours.

In a food processor, place the remaining warm milk, the egg yolks, the tarragon, sugar, the cayenne pepper and a pinch of salt. Process until the ingredients are well mixed. Add the mixture to the yeast batter and mix well.

In another bowl, beat the egg whites until firm. Fold the egg whites into the batter. Let the batter stand at room temperature for 35 minutes longer.

Lightly oil a griddle or a large skillet over medium-high heat. With a ladle, pour enough batter onto the griddle to make a thin pancake about 3 inches in diameter. Cook until golden brown on the bottom, then turn the blini over with a spatula and cook until golden brown on the other side. Make several pancakes at once. Stack the blini and keep them warm in a 200°F oven until ready to serve. Serve with sour cream.

Unusual Appetizers

❦ Deep-Fried Olives ❦

Serves 6

24 pimento- or caper-stuffed green olives	2 eggs
½ cup all-purpose flour	1 cup seasoned breadcrumbs
	vegetable oil for deep frying

Drain the olives. Pat them dry with paper towels, being careful that the stuffing stays inside.

Spread the flour on a plate. Beat the eggs in a shallow bowl. Spread the breadcrumbs on a plate.

Roll the olives in the flour, then dip them in the beaten eggs, then roll them in the breadcrumbs.

Heat the oil in a deep fryer or deep heavy skillet until it reaches 375°F on a deep-frying thermometer. Carefully drop the olives into the oil and fry for 2 to 3 minutes or until evenly golden brown. Drain on paper towels and serve immediately.

❦ Deep-Fried Basil ❦ Leaves

Serves 6

In the summer, when basil is at its best, serve this simple recipe with smoked salmon or herring and drinks.

¼ teaspoon active dry yeast
1 cup beer, at room
   temperature
¾ teaspoon salt

1½ cups flour, sifted
24 large basil leaves
vegetable oil for deep frying
parsley sprigs, for garnish

In a mixing bowl, dissolve the yeast in 2 tablespoons of beer. Add the remaining beer while beating the mixture with a whisk. Add the salt. Then add the flour all at once, whisking rapidly to make a smooth batter. Cover the bowl with a towel or plate and set aside at room temperature for 3 hours.

Wash the basil leaves and pat them dry with paper towels.

Heat the oil in a deep fryer or deep heavy skillet until it reaches 375°F on a deep-frying thermometer. Holding each basil leaf by its stem, dip it into the batter, being careful not to dip the stem. Carefully drop the leaf in the hot oil and fry until golden brown, frying several leaves at a time. Remove with a wire skimmer, drain on paper towels, and then place on a platter and keep warm in a 200°F oven until all the leaves are fried.

To serve, arrange the leaves on a plate, the stems facing the center. Garnish with parsley sprigs and serve.

Celery Root and Sliced Sable

Serves 4

Celery root is also known as celeriac or knob celery. It is very large, light brown in color, and has an intense celery flavor. It is sliced and eaten raw with dips and in salads, or it can be braised or puréed as a cooked vegetable._

1 large celery root
6 tablespoons olive oil
2 tablespoons vinegar
2 teaspoons strong Dijon
    mustard
1 egg yolk

salt
freshly ground black pepper
8 slices sable
2 red sweet peppers, cut into
    thin strips
1 lime, sliced, for garnish

Peel the celery root and cut it into 3-inch slices. Cut each slice in half. Using the julienne blade of a food processor, reduce the slices to slivers.

Place the julienned celery root in a bowl, cover with boiling water and let stand for 2 minutes. Drain, and rinse well under cold water. Drain again and place in a salad bowl.

To make the dressing, in a bowl mix together the olive oil, vinegar, mustard and egg yolk, and salt and black pepper to taste. Pour the dressing over the celery root, toss and set aside.

Just before serving, place 2 slices of the sable on each individual plate. Surround them with the celery salad and decorate with strips of the red pepper. Garnish with a slice of lime on top of the sable.

❧ Marrow and Potatoes ❧

Serves 4

*F*or my stepfather, marrow was French cuisine's greatest
masterpiece. The following recipe is his. He used to get
pounds and pounds of marrow bones and lovingly
prepare this appetizer for us.

   Beef marrow is easily obtainable. Ask the butcher for
large beef marrow bones, about 3 inches long. You should be
able to see the marrow at both ends of the bones.

   Serve the marrow as an appetizer on top of thick slices of
boiled potato.

4 pounds beef marrow
   bones
1 tablespoon plus
   1 teaspoon kosher salt
4 large boiling potatoes
2 tablespoons margarine

4 shallots, chopped
1 cup red wine vinegar
1 cake silken bean curd
freshly ground black pepper
1 head radicchio
1 tablespoon chopped chives

Wash the marrow bones. Place them in a large pot, cover
them with cold water and add 1 tablespoon of the salt. Bring
to a boil. Lower the heat to medium and cook, uncovered,
for 15 minutes. With a slotted spoon, remove the bones to a
large bowl to cool.

   When the bones are cool to the touch, remove the
marrow and put it on a plate. To remove the marrow
without breaking it, tap the bone against the edge of the
table, then shake the marrow out slowly onto a plate.
Alternatively, pass a thin, flat knife blade along the sides of
the marrow as if unmolding a jelly or a pâté. Refrigerate the
marrow for 25 minutes.

Peel the potatoes. Place them in a saucepan, cover them with cold water and add 1 teaspoon salt. Bring to a boil, reduce the heat and cook for 20 minutes, or until the potatoes are tender but still firm. Drain and place in an ovenproof dish and dot them with the margarine. Keep the potatoes warm in a 200°F oven.

In a medium saucepan, place the shallots and the vinegar. Cook over high heat, uncovered, until the vinegar is reduced by half. Add the bean curd, reduce the heat to very low and beat with a wire whisk until the bean curd resembles a smooth cream. Add salt and black pepper to taste.

Cut the marrow into ¼-inch slices. Add the slices to the bean curd sauce and cook over very low heat just until the marrow is hot.

Line each of 4 individual plates with 2 radicchio leaves. Top with 2 to 3 thick potato slices. Spoon the marrow with the sauce over the potatoes. Sprinkle with chopped chives and serve immediately.

❦ Spanish Toasts ❦

Serves 4

*T*hese toasts are served all over Spain, especially in the South, around 5 o'clock with a glass of red wine. You need good country bread such as Russian rye, sourdough or Italian whole wheat bread.

4 thick slices of country
   bread, about ½" thick
2 tablespoons extra-virgin
   olive oil
2 garlic cloves, peeled and
   cut in two

2 large tomatoes
salt
freshly ground black pepper

Brush the slices of bread on both sides with the olive oil and toast them.

As soon as the toast is done, rub one side of the hot slices with the garlic and then tomato, pressing down so that some of the tomato pulp sticks to the bread. Sprinkle with salt and pepper and serve immediately.

❦ Calf's-Foot Jelly ❦

Serves 8

My sister-in-law is English and I am French, and when we were young there was a certain cooking rivalry between us. Each year one of us cooked Thanksgiving dinner and the other cooked dinner on New Year's Eve. We tried to outdo ourselves each time. But there was one thing that my sister-in-law always made better than anyone I knew—the calf's-foot jelly she served as the appetizer. It was light, tasty and beautiful to look at. She generously gave me her recipe for this book. The aïoli sauce is my own touch.

2 pounds calves' feet, cut into small pieces
6 garlic cloves, crushed
kosher salt
freshly ground black pepper
1 quart cold water
1 cup Beef Stock (see page 46)
2 tablespoons drained tiny capers

1 tablespoon vegetable oil
1 sprig fresh tarragon
4 hard-boiled eggs, halved
1 tablespoon black sesame seeds
1 head Boston lettuce
1 cup Aioli (see page 237)

Wash the calves' feet several times. Drain well.

In a large saucepan, place the calves' feet, ⅔ of the crushed garlic, salt and black pepper to taste and 1 quart cold water. Bring to a boil, skim the surface, then reduce the heat and simmer for 1 hour, or until the flesh falls from the bones.

Place a sieve over a large mixing bowl and pour the contents of the saucepan through the sieve. Pour the liquid back into the saucepan.

With your fingers, remove all the meat from the bones. Discard the bones. (Your hands will feel sticky and messy, but it is the only way to do the job.)

Place the meat, the remaining garlic and the Beef Stock in a food processor. Process until all the ingredients are puréed.

Add the meat mixture to the saucepan with the cooking liquid. Bring to a boil, turn off the heat, correct the seasoning and remove from the heat. Let the mixture cool overnight.

The next day, scrape off and discard the fat that has congealed on top. Heat the mixture again and add the capers.

Brush eight 4-ounce porcelain molds with the vegetable oil. Place 2 tarragon leaves in the bottom of each mold. Sprinkle some black sesame seeds over the leaves. Place a hard-boiled egg half yolk-side down on the tarragon and pour a tablespoonful of the calf's-foot mixture on top. Refrigerate until the jelly has just set, about 10 minutes. Then fill the molds with the remaining jelly. Before this last step, it is very important to mix the jelly well so that all the elements are combined. Refrigerate for several hours.

Garnish each of 8 individual plates with a Boston lettuce leaf. Unmold the calf's-foot jelly on top of the leaf and serve with Aïoli.

❦ Fried Cheese ❦

Serves 6

When we came home famished from a long walk in the snow, "Mademoiselle," our old family governess, would make this dish for us. We would all sit around the fireplace and eat fried cheese, served on a bed of lettuce, with strong Dijon mustard and hot French bread. Years later, in New York, I serve these scrumptious morsels late at night or for lunch on Sundays with soup and a salad.

¼ package compressed yeast or ¼ teaspoon active dry yeast
1 cup beer, at room temperature
1½ cups all-purpose flour
¼ teaspoon salt

2 pounds Swiss cheese, in one piece
vegetable oil for deep frying
2 heads Boston lettuce
freshly ground black pepper
Dijon mustard

In a mixing bowl, dissolve the yeast in 2 tablespoons of the beer; add the remaining beer, beating with a wire whisk. Add the flour and the salt all at once, beating rapidly with the whisk.

Pour the batter into a large mixing bowl, cover and set aside for 1 hour.

Cut the cheese into pieces 2 inches square and about ½-inch thick.

In a deep fryer or deep heavy skillet, heat the oil until it reaches 360°F on a deep-frying thermometer.

Dip the cheese squares into the batter and then fry them until golden brown. Drain on paper towels and keep warm in a low oven until all the cheese is done.

Line a platter with whole lettuce leaves. Place 2 cheese pieces on each leaf. Sprinkle with black pepper and serve immediately with strong Dijon mustard.

❦ Gherkin Croutons ❦

Serves 6

*T*hese small croutons are perfect with drinks.

4 tablespoons unsalted
  butter, at room
  temperature
4 hard-boiled eggs
¼ cup grated imported
  Parmesan cheese

salt
freshly ground black pepper
vegetable oil for frying
12 thin slices French bread
8 small sour gherkins

Cut the butter into small pieces and place them in a bowl.
Cut the eggs in half and remove the yolks. Add the yolks to
the butter. Add the cheese, a little salt and freshly ground
black pepper. With a fork, mash the ingredients until
smooth.

In a large skillet, heat the oil over high heat. When the oil
is hot, add the bread and fry until the slices are browned on
both sides. Drain on paper towels and cool. Spread the butter
mixture on the fried bread.

Push the egg whites through a sieve. Slice the gherkins
into very thin strips. Make a lattice with the gherkin strips on
top of the butter and decorate the edges with the egg whites.

❦ Mackerel in Salt ❦

Serves 4

*P*aris has succumbed to the Japanese love of raw fish. In Parisian cafes, you can now order marinated uncooked mackerel. This is an old Turkish recipe served Parisian-style, excellent as an appetizer instead of herring. Ask the fishmonger to fillet the mackerel for you, leaving the skin on.

1 large fresh mackerel, filleted
3 cups coarse kosher salt
1 cup olive oil
1 bay leaf, crushed
freshly ground black pepper
12 small lettuce leaves
2 limes, cut in wedges

Cut each mackerel fillet into bite-sized pieces.

In a deep oval dish, spread half the coarse salt in an even layer. Place the pieces of mackerel on top and cover with the remaining salt. Refrigerate for 48 hours.

In a small bowl, mix the olive oil with the crushed bay leaf. Add freshly ground black pepper to taste and set aside.

To serve, remove the mackerel pieces from the salt. Brush off any excess salt. Cut each lettuce leaf in two. Line a serving dish with the lettuce and place the pieces of mackerel on top. Serve with lime wedges and the spiced oil. Each guest picks up a lettuce leaf with mackerel and dips it in the oil, then sprinkles a few drops of lime juice on it before eating.

Soups

Stocks

❧ Vegetable Stock ❧

Makes 2 quarts

*U*se vegetable stock as a base for sauces and as an alternative to chicken stock. It can be frozen in 1-pint containers for future use or refrigerated for 2 to 3 days.

1 tablespoon vegetable oil
1 large onion, sliced
3 quarts water
3 turnips, peeled and quartered
2 carrots, scraped and sliced
2 celery stalks, cut into 1-inch pieces
2 parsnips, peeled, halved lengthwise and cut into 1-inch pieces

¼ pound string beans
¼ head green cabbage, shredded
2 thyme sprigs or ¼ teaspoon dried thyme
1 bay leaf
10 black peppercorns
salt
freshly ground black pepper

In a 4-quart saucepan, heat the oil over medium heat. Add the onion and sauté until transparent. Add the water, bring to a boil and add all the remaining ingredients. Bring to a boil again, reduce the heat and skim the foam from the surface. Simmer, covered, for 1 hour.

Pour the soup through a strainer placed over a large saucepan. Discard the vegetables. Add salt and black pepper to taste.

❦ Dashi ❦

Serves 4; makes 1 quart

Dashi is the basic Japanese stock made with dried kelp (a seaweed) and shaved dried bonito flakes. The kelp comes in sheets 4 inches by 6 inches; you just need half of a sheet to make the stock. The bonito comes in cellophane bags of about 4 ounces; keep it in a dry place after opening the bag.

These ingredients are available in all health stores and oriental supermarkets.

This versatile stock does not have a strong fish taste. It is excellent to use for soups, for sauces or for basting chicken or fish.

1 quart cold water
1 ounce kelp

1 ounce dried bonito flakes

Fill a medium saucepan with water and add the kelp. Bring the water to a boil over medium heat. Boil for 2 minutes and remove the kelp. Bring the water to a boil again and add ¼ cup cold water to bring the temperature down, immediately add the bonito flakes and bring back to a boil. As soon as the water boils, remove from the heat.

Allow the flakes to fall to the bottom of the saucepan. Remove the foam, then filter the soup through cheese cloth or a very fine sieve.

The stock is ready to use or can be stored in the refrigerator for several days.

❦ Beef Stock ❦

Makes 4 quarts

The secrets of a good beef stock are slow cooking and veal marrow bones. The veal bones give the soup its rich taste; the soy sauce gives it color.

1½ pounds beef shins
1½ pounds veal marrow
   bones
1½ pounds beef brisket
4 garlic cloves, slivered
3 tablespoons vegetable oil
5 quarts water
2 tablespoons kosher salt
6 black peppercorns
2 celery stalks, split down
   the center and cut into
   1-inch pieces

2 carrots, scraped and cut
   into 1-inch pieces
2 onions, each stuck with
   1 clove
2 sprigs fresh thyme or
   1 teaspoon dried thyme
2 parsley sprigs
2 bay leaves
2 tablespoons dark soy
   sauce (optional)

Wash the beef shins and the veal bones under cold running water.

With a sharp knife, make slits in the beef brisket and insert the garlic slivers.

In a large heavy pot, heat the oil over medium-high heat. Add the beef shins and brisket and sauté until browned on all sides. Add the marrow bones and the water. Bring the water slowly to a boil, skimming off the foam that rises to the top. Lower the heat, add the salt and peppercorns and simmer, covered, for 1 hour.

Add the celery, carrots, onions, thyme, parsley and bay leaves. Bring the soup to a boil again, reduce the heat and simmer for 2 hours.

Let the stock cool, covered, at room temperature overnight.

Remove the congealed fat on top of the stock. Add the soy sauce. Reheat the stock slowly over low heat. Remove the beef shins, brisket and veal bones. Discard the shins and bones; reserve the brisket for another use.

Pour the stock through a fine sieve into 1-quart plastic containers. Cover and freeze for future use. The stock will keep in the refrigerator for 3 to 4 days.

❦ Court Bouillon ❦

Makes 6 cups

This simplest of vegetable stocks is a favorite medium for poaching, particularly fish. It will keep for several days in a jar in the refrigerator and can be frozen, too. But it is so quick and easy to make that I usually prepare it fresh for each use.

2 small onions, each stuck
    with 2 cloves
2 shallots, sliced
1 carrot, scraped and sliced
1 garlic clove, crushed
1½ quarts water
½ cup dry white wine

4 tablespoons white wine
    vinegar
1 bay leaf
1 sprig fresh thyme
salt
5 black peppercorns

In a large, deep skillet, combine all the ingredients. Bring to a boil, reduce the heat and simmer for 20 minutes. Strain out the solids before using the bouillon.

❦ Fish Stock ❦

Makes 2 quarts

*A*sk the fishmonger to give you one or two fish heads and some bone trimmings. If he has none, buy two or more small porgies or any other cheap fish to use for making the stock.

2 pounds of fish heads and
   bone trimmings,
   chopped, or 3 porgies,
   cleaned and washed
2 quarts water
5 whole black peppercorns
1 onion, stuck with a clove
2 parsley sprigs

2 fresh thyme sprigs or
   ½ teaspoon dried thyme
2 large carrots, sliced
1 celery stalk, cut in
   1-inch pieces
kosher salt
freshly ground black pepper

In a large pot, place the fish heads and bones. Add the water and bring to a boil. Reduce the heat to medium and skim off the froth. Cover and simmer for 10 minutes.

Add the carrots, onion, celery, parsley, thyme, peppercorns and 1½ teaspoons kosher salt. Bring to a boil, reduce the heat, skim the surface again and simmer, covered, for 30 minutes.

Strain the stock through a very fine sieve placed over another saucepan. Discard the vegetables and fish heads.

Correct the seasoning, adding salt and pepper to taste, and cool to room temperature.

Pour the stock in 1-quart plastic containers and either refrigerate or freeze.

❦ Chicken Stock ❦

Makes 3 quarts

*E*verybody's grandmother makes the best chicken soup, guaranteed to get rid of your flu. I think my chicken soup is excellent, although I am not yet a grandmother. I don't promise that it will cure your cold, but it certainly will lift your spirits.

1 3-pound chicken, quartered
1 pound veal bones
4 leeks, white parts only, tied together with kitchen string
2 medium carrots, scraped
2 turnips, peeled and quartered
1 large onion stuck with 2 cloves
½ pound snow peas
1 large garlic clove
bouquet garni
kosher salt
1 teaspoon black peppercorns

Fill a 5-quart saucepan with cold water. Add the chicken and the veal bones. Bring to a boil, lower the heat and cook for 20 minutes, skimming the surface from time to time.

Add the leeks, carrots, turnips, onion, snow peas, garlic, bouquet garni, peppercorns and kosher salt to taste. Bring to a boil again, then lower the heat and simmer, uncovered, for 1 hour.

Remove the chicken pieces and save them for another use. Strain the soup through a fine sieve into another saucepan. Discard the vegetables and solids remaining in the sieve. Let cool and then refrigerate overnight.

The next day, skim all the fat from the surface of the soup. Reheat the soup and correct the seasoning. You can freeze the soup in 1-quart plastic containers until ready to use.

Vegetable Soups

Cauliflower Soup with Chicken Sauce

Serves 6

If you have followed the recipe for Roast Chicken with Shiitake Mushrooms on page 168, you are left with 2 cups of sauce. Refrigerate the sauce overnight. The next day the fat will have risen to the top and congealed. Discard the fat (this is very easily done with a spatula—the fat just lifts off). You will be left with a rich, dark brown jelly that makes a wonderful soup. In this recipe I add cauliflower, but it could be replaced by celery, mushrooms or any other vegetable.

1 large head cauliflower
2 cups Chicken Sauce (see page 168)
4 cups water
16 fresh medium basil leaves or 1 teaspoon dried basil
salt
freshly ground black pepper
zest of 1 lime, finely julienned
6 slices Italian bread
2 garlic cloves, halved
1 tablespoon olive oil

Trim away the tough stems of the cauliflower. Cut the head into small florets.

In a large pot, place the cauliflower, Chicken Sauce and water. Bring to a boil, lower the heat and cook for 15 minutes.

With a slotted spoon, remove the pieces of cauliflower and place them in a food processor. Add 2 cups of the soup and 10 of the basil leaves. Process until the ingredients are puréed.

Pour the purée back into the soup kettle. Add salt and black pepper to taste (the chicken sauce is already salted, so taste it first before adding more).

Add the lime zest to the soup and simmer for 5 minutes.

Toast the bread. While the bread is still hot, rub it with garlic. Brush some olive oil on each piece.

Pour the soup into 6 individual soup bowls. Garnish each bowl with a basil leaf and serve with the toast.

Cold Avocado and Yogurt Soup

Serves 6

1 avocado, peeled, pitted and sliced
24 ounces plain yogurt
1 cup Vegetable Stock (see page 44)
1 1-inch piece ginger, chopped, or ½ teaspoon dried ground ginger

3 tablespoons lemon juice
¼ teaspoon ground cumin
salt
freshly ground black pepper
3 tablespoons black lumpfish caviar
2 tablespoons chopped fresh mint

Place the avocado slices, 8 ounces of the yogurt, the vegetable stock and ginger in a food processor. Process until the ingredients are puréed. Pour the purée into a large bowl.

In another bowl, beat the remaining yogurt with a fork; add it to the soup. Add the lemon juice, cumin and salt and black pepper to taste. Mix well. Refrigerate for 2 to 3 hours before serving.

Pour the soup into 6 individual soup bowls. Decorate each bowl with ½ tablespoon caviar and some chopped mint.

51

❧ Cauliflower Soup ❧ with Cranberries

Serves 6

*A*round Thanksgiving, cranberries abound and cranberry sauce becomes part of every menu. For a change from the usual fare, try this recipe, which uses tart cranberries to counterbalance the sweetness of the cauliflower and make the soup look beautiful.

1 head cauliflower
1½ quarts Chicken Stock
   (see page 49) or water
2 sprigs fresh rosemary or
   ½ teaspoon dried
   rosemary
2 cups cranberries

½ cup sugar
½ cup water
2 tablespoons chopped
   parsley
salt
freshly ground black pepper

Trim away the hard core of the cauliflower and separate it into florets. Place the cauliflower in a large saucepan, add the Chicken Stock, and bring to a boil. Reduce the heat to medium, add the rosemary and cook for 25 minutes or until the cauliflower is easily pierced with a fork. Set aside.

Place the cranberries in a saucepan; add the sugar and the water. Bring to a boil and cook over high heat for 3 to 4 minutes or until the cranberries all pop. Remove from the heat.

Remove the rosemary sprigs from the cauliflower. Purée the cauliflower with the stock in a food processor, in batches if necessary. Pour the soup back into the saucepan. Add the parsley and salt and black pepper to taste.

Gently heat the soup just before serving. Fill the individual serving bowls and add about 1 tablespoon of the cranberries to the center of the bowl.

Fresh Summer Pea Soup

Serves 6

In late June, peas are at their best. In this soup I also use some of the small, tender pods, which add a distinct flavor. If you use frozen peas, add 2 or 3 parsley stems in place of the pods.

4 pounds fresh peas, in the pods, or 1 10-ounce package frozen tiny peas (petits pois)
6 cups water
1 tablespoon salt
4 cups Dashi (see page 45) or Vegetable Stock (see page 44)

½ cup heavy cream
1 2-inch piece fresh ginger, grated, or ½ teaspoon dried ground ginger
freshly ground black pepper
parsley sprigs, for garnish

Shell the peas. Set aside 20 of the smallest pods and ½ cup of the shelled peas.

In a large saucepan, place the remaining peas and the reserved pods. Add 4 cups of the water and salt and bring to a boil. Reduce the heat to medium and cook, uncovered, for 20 minutes. Drain the peas and the pods.

Place the peas and the pods in a food processor with ½ cup of the Dashi and process until puréed. Strain through a very fine strainer placed over a saucepan.

Add the remaining Dashi and the heavy cream to the purée. Mix well and add the ginger and black pepper to taste.

In a small saucepan, bring the remaining water to a boil; add the reserved peas, bring to a boil again and turn off the heat. Let stand 3 minutes and then drain well.

Add the peas to the soup. Heat gently and serve garnished with the parsley sprigs.

53

ᘛ Artichoke Soup with ᘚ Fresh Salmon Caviar

Serves 6

*T*his elegant recipe is made with fresh artichokes, but if you are in a hurry you can replace them with canned artichoke hearts.

2 quarts water
4 large artichokes
1 onion
bouquet garni
2 tablespoons vegetable oil
6 shallots, chopped
3 garlic cloves, chopped

2 tablespoons all-purpose flour
salt
freshly ground black pepper
1 tablespoon unsalted butter (optional)
¼ pound fresh salmon caviar

In a large stock pot, bring the water to a boil. Add the artichokes, onion and bouquet garni. Bring to a boil again, reduce the heat to medium and cook for 20 minutes or until an artichoke leaf pulls off easily. With a slotted spoon, transfer the artichokes to a colander and rinse well under cold running water. Drain well. Reserve the cooking liquid.

When the artichokes are cool enough to handle, remove all the leaves (reserve them to serve with the classic Vinaigrette on page 000). With a teaspoon, remove the inedible chokes. Using the julienne blade of a food processor, julienne the artichoke hearts; set them aside.

Boil the reserved artichoke cooking liquid until it is reduced by about one-fourth, to about 6 cups.

In a medium skillet, heat the oil over medium heat. Add the shallots and the garlic and cook, stirring with a wooden spoon, for 5 minutes. Add the flour and stir briskly until the flour is a light golden brown; slowly add 1 cup of the artichoke stock, stirring constantly. Pour the flour-and-shallot mixture into the saucepan with the artichoke stock. Add the julienned artichoke hearts and salt and black pepper to taste. Simmer for 3 minutes; do not let the soup boil. Add the butter, if desired.

To serve, pour the soup into 6 individual bowls. Using a tablespoon and a butter knife, slide a spoonful of the caviar into the center of each bowl. Serve immediately.

❧ Cream of Tomato Soup with Mint ❧

Serves 6

3 pounds fresh beefsteak
  tomatoes
2 tablespoons olive oil
1 leek, white part only,
  sliced
2 garlic cloves, chopped
1 tablespoon chopped
  parsley
1 sprig thyme or
  ⅛ teaspoon dried thyme

1½ quarts Vegetable Stock
  (see page 44)
1 teaspoon sugar
2 tablespoons chopped fresh
  mint or 1 teaspoon dried
  mint
salt
freshly ground black pepper
¼ cup sour cream
6 mint leaves, for garnish

Place the tomatoes in a bowl with enough boiling water to cover; leave them for 2 minutes. Drain and rinse well under cold running water. Peel, quarter and seed the tomatoes. Set them aside in a bowl.

In a medium saucepan, heat the olive oil over medium heat. Add the leek and the garlic; cook for 2 minutes. Add the tomatoes, parsley and thyme and simmer for 5 minutes.

Add the Vegetable Stock and sugar. Bring to a boil, reduce the heat and simmer for 15 minutes.

Remove the thyme. Pour the soup into a food processor and purée, in batches if necessary. Pour the purée back into the saucepan and add the chopped mint and salt and black pepper to taste; bring to a boil and then turn off the heat.

Pour the soup into 6 individual soup bowls. Add 1 tablespoon of sour cream to each bowl and garnish with a mint leaf.

Vegetable Soup with Basil Sauce

Serves 6

Soup:
2 quarts water
1 medium onion, stuck with
    2 cloves
1 bay leaf
1 pound potatoes, peeled
    and diced
3 carrots, scraped and diced
4 medium turnips, peeled
    and diced

½ pound string beans,
    trimmed and halved
2 leeks, white parts only,
    thinly sliced
½ pound tomatoes, peeled,
    seeded and diced
¼ pound fresh peas
salt
freshly ground black pepper

Basil Sauce:
36 fresh medium basil leaves
2 garlic cloves
3 tablespoons olive oil
2 tablespoons unsalted
    butter

salt
freshly ground black pepper

6 slices Italian bread

In a large saucepan, bring the water to a boil. Add the onion and bay leaf, lower the heat to medium and cook for 5 minutes.

Add the potatoes and the carrots and cook for 10 minutes. (Each time you add a vegetable to the soup, the water will stop boiling. Count the cooking time from the moment the water starts to boil again.) Add the turnips, string beans and leeks and cook for another 10 minutes. Add the tomatoes, peas and salt and black pepper to taste. Cook for 20 minutes longer. Remove the soup from the heat and keep warm.

Set aside 6 of the basil leaves for garnish. Place the remaining basil in a food processor. Add the garlic, olive oil, butter and salt and black pepper to taste. Process until the ingredients are puréed. Pour the mixture into a bowl.

Pour the soup into 6 individual soup bowls. Float a tablespoon of the basil sauce in the center of each bowl. Garnish with a basil leaf and serve with the toasted Italian bread.

Beef and Chicken Soups

Thanksgiving Turkey Soup

Serves 6

*T*wo days after Thanksgiving, when everyone is done picking at the turkey carcass, is the time to make this great soup—a meal in itself.

1 turkey carcass, cut into
  several pieces
2 quarts water
1 onion, stuck with 2 cloves
1 cup pearl barley
1 ounce dried Polish
  mushrooms
1 3-inch piece fresh ginger,
  peeled and halved
3 carrots, scraped and cut
  into 2-inch pieces
3 celery stalks, cut into
  1-inch pieces
1 acorn squash, peeled and
  quartered

salt
freshly ground black pepper
2 8-ounce cans artichoke
  hearts, drained
1 1-pound can chick peas,
  drained
1 1-pound can peeled Italian
  tomatoes, drained
2 tablespoons olive oil
2 garlic cloves, finely
  chopped
8 thick slices black bread

Place the turkey carcass in an 8-quart soup pot. Cover with water and bring to a boil. Skim the foam from the surface. Add the onion, lower the heat to medium, cover and cook for 15 minutes.

Add the barley, dried mushrooms, ginger, carrots, celery, acorn squash and salt and black pepper to taste. Bring to a boil, lower the heat and cook for 20 minutes.

Cut the artichoke hearts in half. Add them to the soup. Add the chick peas and cook for another 10 minutes. Remove and discard the turkey carcass.

Add the tomatoes to the soup and simmer for 5 minutes. Turn off the heat and let the soup stand for 1 hour or more.

Preheat the broiler or toaster oven.

In a small bowl, mix the olive oil with the garlic. Brush some of the mixture on the black bread slices and place them under the broiler or in the toaster oven for 15 seconds.

Reheat the soup just before serving. Serve in large bowls with the toasted black bread.

❧ Lentil Soup ❧

Serves 8

1 pound brown lentils
about 1½ quarts Chicken
  Stock (see page 49)
1 onion, stuck with 1 clove
2 bay leaves
salt

freshly ground black pepper
3 tablespoons olive oil
4 garlic cloves, sliced
6 kosher frankfurters, thinly
  sliced

Place the lentils in a large saucepan. Add the Chicken Stock, bring to a boil, and lower the heat. Add the onion, bay leaves and salt and black pepper to taste. Simmer, covered, for 1 hour or until the lentils are tender, add a little more chicken stock if the lentils start to get too thick or stick to the bottom of the saucepan.

Put 2 cups of drained lentils into a food processor and purée. Pour the purée back into the lentil soup.

In a small skillet, heat the oil over medium-high heat. Add the garlic and sauté until golden brown. Pour the oil and garlic into the soup. Add the frankfurters and cook for 5 minutes. Turn off the heat and let the soup stand for at least 1 hour (the soup is even better if it is left overnight).

To serve, gently reheat the soup. Serve from a soup terrine with crackers.

Kasha Soup with Poached Egg

Serves 6

1 tablespoon vegetable oil
1 large onion, chopped
1 egg
1 cup fine-grain kasha
2 quarts Beef Stock (see page 46)
1 teaspoon grated lemon zest

salt
freshly ground black pepper
12 sprigs curly parsley
vegetable oil for frying
6 Poached Eggs (see page 87)

In a large skillet, heat the oil over medium heat. Add the onion and sauté until it is light brown, stirring constantly. Remove from the heat and set aside.

In a mixing bowl, beat the egg. Add the kasha and mix well to coat all the grains. Add the kasha to the onions and cook over medium heat, stirring constantly, until the kasha grains are separate and dry. Add 2 cups of the beef stock, lemon zest and salt and black pepper to taste. Cover and simmer for 10 minutes or until the kasha is fluffy and tender. Set aside.

In a large saucepan, heat the remaining beef stock. Add the kasha and keep warm while frying the parsley.

Wash the parsley sprigs and pat them dry with paper towels. In a small skillet, heat ¼ inch of oil until it is very hot. Add the parsley sprigs and fry for 1 minute. Drain on paper towels.

To serve, pour the hot soup into 6 individual soup bowls. Add a Poached Egg to each bowl and garnish with 2 fried parsley sprigs. Serve immediately.

ꙮ Naima's Matzo Ball ꙮ Soup

Serves 6

⅓ cup vegetable oil
1 large onion, diced
4 eggs, separated
½ cup plus 1½ quarts
   Chicken Stock (see page
   49)
1 cup matzo meal

½ cup diced cooked beef
   marrow (see page 000)
salt
freshly ground black pepper
2 quarts salted water
6 parsley sprigs, for garnish

In a skillet, heat the oil over medium heat. Add the onion and cook until it is transparent but not browned. Set aside.

In a large bowl, beat the egg yolks. Add the ½ cup Chicken Stock and beat again. Add the matzo meal, diced marrow and salt and black pepper to taste. Mix well with a wooden spoon. Add the onions and the oil and mix well.

In a large bowl, beat the egg whites with a pinch of salt until they are firm. Fold the egg whites into the matzo mixture and refrigerate for 4 to 5 hours. Form the mixture into balls the size of a walnut—about 1 inch in diameter. The balls will expand when cooked.

In a large saucepan, bring the salted water to a rapid boil. Drop in the matzo balls. Bring back to a boil, reduce the heat, cover tightly and cook for 30 minutes. Remove the matzo balls from the water and keep warm.

Heat the 1½ quarts chicken soup in a saucepan until very hot.

Place 2 matzo balls in each of six individual soup bowls. Add the Chicken Stock, garnish with parsley sprigs and serve.

❧ Spaghetti ❧ Squash Soup

Serves 6

1 large spaghetti squash,
about 3 pounds
3 marrow bones
2 quarts Chicken Stock (see
page 49)
salt

freshly ground black pepper
1 loaf Italian bread
½ cup Aïoli (see page 237)
2 tablespoons chopped
parsley, for garnish

In a large saucepan, put the spaghetti squash and cover it with boiling water; bring to a boil, add the marrow bones and cook for 20 minutes, or until the spaghetti squash is easily pierced with a fork. With a spatula, carefully remove the marrow bones. Remove the marrow by tapping the bones against the edge of a plate; the marrow will easily slide out. Cover the marrow and refrigerate. Remove the spaghetti squash and cut it in half. Remove the flesh with a fork and set aside.

In a saucepan, heat the stock. Add the strands of spaghetti squash to the stock. Add salt and black pepper to taste and simmer for 5 minutes.

Remove the marrow from the refrigerator and cut it into 12 slices.

Cut the Italian bread into 6 slices and toast them. Spread each slice with some Aïoli.

To serve the soup, put 2 marrow slices in each individual serving bowl. Pour the very hot soup over them and sprinkle with the parsley. Serve with the toast on the side.

Carrot and Sweet Potato Tzimmes Soup

Serves 6

3 tablespoons vegetable oil
3 medium onions, quartered
3½ cups Chicken Stock (see
   page 49) or Vegetable
   Stock (see page 44)
1 pound carrots, scraped
   and cut into 2-inch
   pieces
2 medium sweet potatoes,
   peeled and quartered

salt
1 2-inch piece fresh ginger,
   grated, or ½ teaspoon
   dried ground ginger
freshly ground black pepper
4 teaspoons chopped fresh
   dill

In a large saucepan, heat the oil over medium-high heat; add the onion and sauté until golden and transparent. Add the stock, carrots, sweet potatoes and salt to taste. Bring to a boil, reduce the heat and simmer for 10 minutes. Add the ginger and cook for 8 minutes longer, or until the carrots are easily pierced with a fork.

Purée the soup in a food processor, in batches if necessary. Return the soup to the saucepan, add salt and black pepper to taste and 1 teaspoon of the chopped dill.

Heat the soup gently; do not let it boil. Garnish with the remaining chopped dill and serve.

❧ Fennel and Mustard ❧ Greens Soup

Serves 6

*M*ustard greens were neglected until recently because for a very long time they were considered a poor man's vegetable. Today they are finally being appreciated and are now easily obtainable in most supermarkets. From October to December mustard greens are tender, not bitter, and make excellent soup. As a braised vegetable, they are a piquant contrast to lamb or fish.*

2 medium fennels
1 pound mustard greens
3 potatoes, peeled and
   quartered
3 scallions, cut into 1-inch
   pieces

1 sprig fresh rosemary
1½ quarts Chicken Stock
   (see page 49) or Beef
   Stock (see page 46)
salt
freshly ground black pepper

Trim the fennel bulbs, reserving some of the feathery leaves for garnish. Quarter the bulbs and place them in a large pot. Add the mustard greens, potatoes, scallions and rosemary. Add stock, bring to a boil, lower the heat and simmer, covered, for 30 minutes.

With a slotted spoon, remove the vegetables and place them in a food processor. Add ½ cup of the liquid and process until the ingredients are puréed.

Pour the purée back into the pot. Add salt and black pepper to taste.

Just before serving, gently reheat the soup. Pour the soup into 6 individual soup bowls and garnish with the fennel leaves.

Split-Pea Soup with Grated Daikon

Serves 6

½ pound split green peas, soaked at least 2 hours in cold water
2 quarts Chicken Stock (see page 49)
2 garlic cloves, chopped
2 onions, stuck with 1 clove
2 carrots, scraped and thinly sliced

2 celery stalks, thinly sliced
1 bay leaf
1 teaspoon dried thyme
1 daikon, peeled and grated
2 tablespoons chopped wakame or nori (dried seaweed)

Drain the split peas. In a large saucepan, place the peas and add the Chicken Stock, garlic, onions, carrots, celery, bay leaf and thyme. Bring to a boil, reduce the heat to medium, skim the foam from the surface and simmer, covered, for 1 hour, stirring occasionally.

Discard the bay leaf. Pour the soup into a food processor, in batches, if necessary, and add the bean curd. Purée the soup and pour it back into the saucepan. Keep warm until ready to serve.

Pour the soup into 6 individual soup bowls. Carefully place a tablespoon of grated daikon in the center of each bowl. Sprinkle with some chopped wakame and serve.

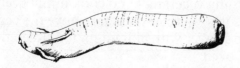

Fish Soups

❧ Fish Soup with ❧ Vegetables

Serves 4

3 quarts Fish Stock (see
  page 48)
4 small carrots, scraped
4 onions, peeled
4 small turnips, peeled
½ pound string beans
4 leeks, white parts only, cut
  into 1-inch pieces
2 zucchini, cut into 1-inch
  pieces
1 head broccoli, florets only
4 small perch cut in two
4 fillets of sole, rolled and
  tied with toothpicks
2 striped bass fillets, about
  6 ounces each

2 small red snappers cut in
  pieces, heads removed
2 tablespoons olive oil
2 tablespoons chopped basil
  or 2 teaspoons dried
  basil
2 tablespoons chopped
  parsley
salt
freshly ground black pepper
4 slices white bread, toasted
2 garlic cloves, halved
4 sprigs of mint

In a large pot, bring the stock to a boil, reduce the heat, add
the carrots, onions and turnips. Cook for 5 minutes, then
add all remaining vegetables and cook until barely tender,
about 10 minutes. With a spatula, remove the vegetables to a
large bowl and cover with aluminum foil. Keep them warm
in a very low oven.

Add the fish to the soup, bring to a boil, reduce the heat and simmer for 10 minutes. Remove the fish to the vegetable bowl and return the bowl to the oven.

In a small saucepan, heat the olive oil over medium heat and add the basil and parsley. Sauté for 1 minute. Pour the oil into the soup and correct the seasoning with salt and pepper.

Rub the toasts with the garlic.

In 4 large bowls, place some vegetables and on top of them pieces of each kind of fish. On top of the fish, place half a piece of toast.

Heat the broth. Pour some into each bowl, garnish with mint leaves, and serve hot with the other half of the toast on the side.

Summer Tomato Soup with Halibut

Serves 6

This soup is especially welcome on a hot summer's day for lunch or supper. Really ripe fresh tomatoes and fresh basil are required. The halibut with tarragon is optional. However, the soup with the fish accompanied by crusty bread and a salad makes a delightful light meal.

3 pounds ripe beefsteak
    tomatoes
12 medium basil leaves
1 teaspoon salt
freshly ground black pepper
4 cups Vegetable Stock (see
    page 44)

2 tablespoons olive oil
4 halibut steaks, about
    1 pound total (optional)
1 tablespoon chopped fresh
    tarragon or ½ teaspoon
    dried
1 lime, thinly sliced

Place the tomatoes in a large bowl and add enough boiling water to cover. Let stand for 5 minutes. Drain and rinse well under cold running water. Drain again. Peel, quarter and seed the tomatoes. Place them in a food processor with 6 basil leaves and salt and black pepper to taste. Process until the ingredients are puréed.

Pour the mixture into a large saucepan. Slowly add the Vegetable Stock, stirring with a wooden spoon. Gently bring the soup to a boil and turn off the heat.

To add the halibut to the soup, in a skillet heat the oil over medium-high heat. Add the halibut steaks and sauté for 3 minutes; turn the steaks and sauté for another 3 minutes. Sprinkle the fish with salt and black pepper to taste and the fresh tarragon. Place the steaks on a plate.

Cut the fish into small pieces and remove any bones. Add the fish to the tomato soup. Gently heat the soup; do not let it boil.

Pour the soup into 6 individual soup bowls. Garnish each bowl with a lime slice and a basil leaf.

Salads

Vegetable Salads

❦ Summer Tomato Salad ❦

Serves 6

*T*he legend in my family is that my husband married me for my tomato salad. He tells anyone who has not heard the story that when he first met me in Paris at my house, I served him the best tomato salad he had ever eaten. To this day, I don't know what was so special about my salad except that I used fresh tomatoes and that it was summer.

1 quart water
bowl of iced water
6 ripe tomatoes
2½ tablespoons extra-virgin
    olive oil
1 tablespoon lemon juice
½ teaspoon salt
freshly ground black pepper
2 garlic cloves, chopped
1 large red onion, thinly
    sliced
1 tablespoon chopped fresh
    tarragon or 1 teaspoon
    dried tarragon

In a large saucepan, bring 1 quart of water to a boil. Remove from the heat and immediately put all the tomatoes into the water (you can put in 2 at a time if you are using a smaller saucepan). After 3 minutes, remove the tomatoes from the hot water with a slotted spoon and plunge them into a large bowl of iced water to cool. Drain well and peel the tomatoes (the skin will slip off very easily). Set the tomatoes aside.

In a bowl, mix together the lemon juice, olive oil, salt and black pepper to taste. Add the garlic and mix well.

Slice the tomatoes over a large salad bowl (so the tomato juice falls into the bowl). Add the onion slices and toss lightly.

Pour the dressing over the tomatoes and sprinkle the tarragon on top. Marinate for 30 minutes before serving.

Three-Color Marinated Beans

Serves 6

1 1-pound can kidney beans, drained
1 1-pound can chick peas, drained
½ pound cooked string beans
½ pound cooked yellow wax beans
1 red onion, thinly sliced

¼ cup vegetable oil
¼ cup olive oil
¼ cup wine vinegar
½ cup sugar
1 teaspoon salt
½ teaspoon freshly ground black pepper
parsley sprigs, for garnish

In a large salad bowl, mix together the kidney beans, chick peas, string beans, wax beans and onion.

In a small bowl, mix together the vegetable oil, olive oil, vinegar, sugar, salt and black pepper. Pour the dressing over the beans and toss. Cover with foil and refrigerate overnight. Serve garnished with parsley sprigs.

🍃 Savoy Salad with 🍃 Cranberries

Serves 6

*S*avoy Salad or flowering kale was developed by John Moore in the Salinas Valley south of San Francisco. The savoy salad belongs to the cabbage family and looks like a giant rose, its leaves deeply hued from white to purple to green. It can be eaten raw in a salad, or steamed or fried. Here it is steamed, and the leaves are sprinkled with cranberries like drops of dew on the savoy salad just before it is picked.

1 cup fresh cranberries
½ cup water
¼ cup sugar
1 large savoy salad
2 tablespoons olive oil
1 tablespoon lime juice

1 garlic clove, chopped
salt
freshly ground black pepper
1 bunch fresh mint, for
  garnish

Place the cranberries in a medium saucepan. Add the water and sugar. Bring to a boil, lower the heat to medium, and cook the cranberries for 6 minutes or until they pop open. Set aside.

Keep the savoy salad whole, but cut off the stem. Wash and drain well in a colander.

Steam the savoy salad in a bamboo or metal steamer for 5 minutes. Remove it and place it upright, stem-side down, on a round platter.

In a small bowl, mix together the olive oil, lime juice, garlic and salt and black pepper to taste. Pour the lime dressing over the savoy salad.

Drain the cranberries and sprinkle them inside and around the savoy salad leaves. Place a bouquet of mint leaves in the center of the cabbage and serve.

Lentil and Red Okra Salad

Serves 6

*R*ed okra, which is much more tender than green okra, is now available in gourmet vegetable and fruit stores and in the special fruit and vegetable sections of supermarkets. Choose small okra; they are more tender and less stringy than the larger ones.

½ pound red okra
4 cups cooked lentils
2 garlic cloves
1 2-inch piece fresh ginger
    root, peeled and
    julienned

3 tablespoons olive oil
1 tablespoon lemon juice
½ tablespoon chopped
    cilantro
salt
freshly ground black pepper

Place the okra in a saucepan and cover them with cold water. Bring to a boil, remove from the heat and drain well. Rinse the okra under cold running water and drain again. Thinly slice the okra.

In a salad bowl, mix together the okra, lentils, garlic and ginger. Mix well.

In a small bowl, mix together the olive oil, lemon juice, cilantro and salt and black pepper to taste. Pour the dressing over the lentils, toss well, and serve.

73

New Potato Salad with Yogurt

Serves 4

When our children were young, we used to spend our summer at the seaside. The window of the kitchen overlooked a large potato field and I used to watch the potato plants slowly mature over the summer months, waiting for the moment I could tell the children: "Today is the day we dig potatoes!" Each of us would grab a large spoon and a basket and off we would go, sloshing through the mud to get the tiniest potatoes we could find, potatoes the size of a walnut.

I would then prepare this recipe, given to me by my grandmother. It's divine! Serve the potatoes as an appetizer when your main course is fish. The success of this dish depends on the yogurt. This is not the time to be on a diet—choose whole-milk natural yogurt.

Today, a good variety of small new potatoes is available year round. One of my favorites is a purple variety now being grown in upstate New York. Surprisingly, it was very common in the nineteenth century, and has only recently made a comeback.

2½ pounds small new potatoes
2 cups plain whole-milk yogurt
¼ teaspoon ground cumin
¼ teaspoon cayenne
salt
freshly ground black pepper

1 large tomato, peeled, seeded and diced
1 medium onion, diced
1 head romaine lettuce, leaves separated
4 tablespoons chopped parsley

In a large saucepan, place the potatoes with enough water to cover. Bring to a boil, reduce the heat and simmer for 25 minutes, or until the potatoes can be easily pierced with a fork. Drain immediately and keep warm in the saucepan while preparing the dressing.

Place the yogurt in a large bowl and add the cumin, cayenne pepper and salt and black pepper to taste. Beat with a fork until the yogurt is very smooth. Add the tomato and onion. Mix well and correct the seasoning.

Line a salad bowl with the romaine lettuce leaves. Add the warm potatoes to the dressing and toss well. Pour into the salad bowl, sprinkle with the chopped parsley and serve with warm whole-wheat Italian bread.

"Daisy" Salad
ॐ of Endive and ॐ
Miniature Beets

Serves 6

A mong the most interesting of the new miniature vegetables now being grown all over America are tiny beets, about the size of a quail's egg or cherry tomato. These beets are sweet as honey. They can be served sauteed with parsley or filled with cream cheese mixed with chives as an appetizer.

In this recipe, the tiny beets are the heart of a giant daisy-shaped arrangement. If miniature beets are not available, you can use sliced kiwi fruit or thin slices of orange with the skins on. If you are very adventurous, try canistel, a new fruit from Florida which looks and tastes somewhat like hard-boiled egg yolk. For this dish you will need a very large round platter.

2 bunches miniature beets, about 1½ pounds

2 pounds Belgian endive

3½ tablespoons olive oil

2 tablespoons lemon juice

2 shallots, finely chopped

salt

freshly ground black pepper

1 bunch chives, for garnish

Trim and discard the leaves and stems from the beets. Wash the beets well. Place them in a saucepan and cover with water. Bring to a boil, cover, and simmer for 20 minutes, or until tender when pierced with a fork. Drain in a colander, then refresh under cold water. Peel the beets (the skins should slide off easily). Sprinkle with salt and set aside.

Quickly wash the endive and pat them dry with paper towels. Separate the leaves.

To make a "daisy" with the endive, make a circle with the larger leaves side-by-side in a circle around the edges of the round platter, with their pointed ends hanging over the rim. Make a second concentric circle, placing a smaller leaf inside a larger one; make a third circle and then a fourth if you haven't used all the leaves. Leave an empty circle in the center of the platter. Mound the beets in the center.

To make the dressing, combine in a small bowl the olive oil, lemon juice, shallots and salt and black pepper to taste. Mix well. Slowly pour the dressing over the endives and the beets. Arrange 5 or 6 chive stalks among the beets to resemble the pistils of a flower. Serve immediately.

Curried Rice Salad with Vegetables

Serves 4

4 cups cooked long-grain rice
½ teaspoon mild curry powder mixed with 2 tablespoons hot water
½ pound cooked string beans
¼ pound frozen tiny green peas
1 3-ounce jar pickled pearl onions (cocktail onions), drained

6 red radishes, sliced
2 celery stalks, diced
2 Japanese cucumbers, sliced
1 sweet red pepper, diced
½ cup Crème Fraîche (see page 231) or sour cream
2 tablespoons lime juice
1 tablespoon olive oil
salt
freshly ground black pepper

Place the rice in a salad bowl. Pour the curry mixture over it and toss well.

Cut the string beans in half crosswise and place them in another bowl.

Plunge the peas into a saucepan of boiling water, turn off the heat and let the peas stay in the water 3 minutes. Drain and add them to the string beans. Add the pearl onions, radishes, celery, cucumbers and red pepper.

In a small bowl, beat together the Crème Fraîche, lime juice and olive oil. Add salt and black pepper to taste. Add to the vegetables and toss well; then add the vegetables to the rice and toss the salad.

Poultry Salads

❧ Turkey Salad ❧

Serves 4

After two days, leftover turkey can be taxing to anyone's imagination. This salad should be made just before you are about to give up and throw the leftovers into a soup.

½ pound small white
   mushrooms
3 tablespoons lemon juice
1 pink grapefruit, peeled
½ head green cabbage,
   finely julienned
3 cups leftover turkey,
   coarsely diced

3 celery stalks, diced
½ cup Classic Vinaigrette
   (see page 230)
¼ teaspoon grated ginger or
   ⅛ teaspoon dried
   ground ginger
2 tablespoons chopped
   parsley

Remove the mushroom stems and set them aside for another use. Wash the mushroom caps and pat them dry with paper towels. Sprinkle the mushrooms with the lemon juice to keep them from discoloring.

Peel the grapefruit and break it into segments. Remove all the white pith from the segments and cut them in half.

Line a salad bowl with the cabbage.

In another bowl, place the mushrooms, turkey, celery and grapefruit segments.

In a small bowl, stir together the Vinaigrette and ginger. Add the parsley. Pour the vinaigrette over the turkey mixture and toss well. Place the turkey salad on top of the cabbage.

🍓 Chicory Salad with 🍓 Chicken and Figs

Serves 6

*C*hicory is a salad green with very narrow, frizzy-edged leaves. Indeed, the word for chicory in French is frisée. When buying chicory, look for heads with bright yellow inner leaves. Discard the outer green leaves, which can be tough. The tender inner leaves go beautifully with the chicken and figs in this salad. I suggest you serve it with a loaf of fresh black bread.

1 large or 2 medium heads
   chicory
6 fresh figs
2 poached chicken breasts,
   shredded

1 tablespoon chopped chives
¼ cup Classic Vinaigrette
   (see page 00)

Wash the chicory and remove and discard all tough outer leaves. Separate the inner leaves and pat them dry with paper towels. Place the leaves in a salad bowl.

Peel the figs and cut them into quarters without cutting through the base. Place the figs in the salad bowl.

Arrange the strips of chicken breast between the figs. Sprinkle the salad with the chopped chives. Pour the Vinaigrette over the salad and serve.

Fish Salads

❧ Mrs. Winterbottom's ❧
Haddock Salad

Serves 4

Mrs. Winterbottom was a very prim old lady who lived in Dodoma, Tanzania. Food was scarce, but Mrs. Winterbottom always managed to serve her guests unusual and delicious meals. One night she called to invite us for dinner, adding, "My dear, I just received some smoked haddock from England and I will make you my mother's haddock salad!" "I don't like haddock," said my son; "Nor do I," added my husband. But we all liked Mrs. Winterbottom; so we went, expecting the worst. And the meal was delicious! My son had double helpings and my husband flirted with old Mrs. Winterbottom. She was so pleased, she gave me the recipe, and I promised to put it in my book.

2 cups water
1 cup milk
1 pound smoked haddock
6 large potatoes, boiled and
   peeled
2½ tablespoons olive oil
1 tablespoon lemon juice

1 tablespoon drained capers
freshly ground black pepper
½ cup shelled chopped
   walnuts
½ tablespoon chopped fresh
   dill

In a large skillet, combine the water and the milk. Bring to a boil and add the haddock; bring to a boil again, reduce the heat and cook for 15 minutes.

With a spatula, remove the haddock to a plate.

Slice the potatoes and place them in a salad bowl.

With two forks, remove the bones from the haddock and flake the fish. Add the haddock to the potatoes.

In a small bowl, mix together the oil, lemon juice, capers and black pepper to taste. Mix well. You need no salt, as the haddock is salty.

Pour the dressing over the haddock and potatoes and toss well. Scatter the walnuts over the salad and sprinkle with the dill. Serve tepid.

Italian-Style Rice Salad with Tuna

Serves 6

4 cups cooked long-grain rice

1 6-ounce can Italian dark tuna in oil

1 green pepper

4 anchovies, coarsely chopped

¼ cup Classic Vinaigrette (see page 230)

1 teaspoon Dijon mustard

2 tomatoes, thinly sliced

2 hard-boiled eggs, sliced

1 tablespoon chopped chives

Place the rice in a large salad bowl.

In another bowl, place the tuna with the oil. With a fork, separate the tuna into bite-sized flakes.

Cut the green pepper into long, thin strips. Cut each strip in two and add them to the tuna. Add the anchovies.

In a small bowl, mix the Vinaigrette with the mustard. Add to the tuna and mix well. Add the tuna to the rice and toss the salad.

To serve, garnish the salad with alternate slices of tomato and hard-boiled egg. Sprinkle with chives and serve.

81

Molded Rice Salad
꒐ with Tuna and ꒐
Vegetables

Serves 6

*M*âche or corn salad is a short stalk with 3 or 4 small, dark-green leaves. It is sold by the pound; a few ounces are usually sufficient. Mâche can be replaced by watercress or Bibb lettuce.

2 tablespoons vegetable oil
2 cups long-grain rice
4 cups water
salt
freshly ground black pepper
1 6½-ounce can water-
   packed tuna
2 cooked carrots, diced
½ pound cooked string
   beans, diced

2 tablespoons chopped fresh
   basil or 1 teaspoon dried
   basil
2 cups Mayonnaise (see
   page 240)
½ teaspoon lemon juice
4 ounces mâche

Heat 1 tablespoon of the oil in a large saucepan. When the oil is hot, add the rice and cook for 2 minutes, stirring constantly. Add the water and salt and black pepper to taste. Bring to a boil, reduce the heat and simmer, covered, for 20 minutes or until the rice is done. Cool in the refrigerator.

Drain the tuna and break it into small flakes. In a bowl, mix together the tuna, carrots and string beans. Add the basil and salt and pepper to taste. Add the cold rice and mix well. Then add the Mayonnaise and mix well.

Oil a 5-cup ceramic savarin mold. Fill the mold with the rice, pressing it down with the back of a soup spoon. Refrigerate for 2 to 3 hours.

In a small bowl, mix together the lemon juice and the remaining oil. Add salt and pepper to taste and mix well. Toss the mâche with the dressing.

To serve, unmold the rice salad onto a round platter. Fill the center with the mâche salad and serve.

Hot Potato Salad with Herring and Beets

Serves 6

*S*erve this with thick slices of fresh black pumpernickel.

1 ½ pounds small red
   potatoes
1 teaspoon salt
2 sweet-pickled herring
   fillets, cut into bite-sized
   pieces
1 medium onion, sliced

1 sour pickle, sliced
¾ cup drained canned baby
   beets
½ cup Classic Vinaigrette
   (see page 230)
1 teaspoon Dijon mustard

Place the unpeeled potatoes in a saucepan; cover with cold water and add the salt. Bring to a boil, reduce the heat to medium and cook for 20 minutes, uncovered, or until the potatoes are easily pierced with a fork. Drain the potatoes. Using a knife and fork, cut each potato in half and place in a salad bowl.

Add the herring, onion, pickle and whole baby beets.

In a small bowl, mix the Vinaigrette with the Dijon mustard. Pour the dressing over the potatoes and gently toss the salad.

83

Salad with Sole and Smoked Salmon

Serves 4

2 8-ounce sole fillets
2 large slices smoked salmon
2 cups Court Bouillon (see
   page 47)
1 cucumber
6 red cabbage leaves
1 teaspoon chopped chives

1 tablespoon pine nuts
½ cake silken tofu (bean
   curd)
1 teaspoon wine vinegar
1 shallot, coarsely chopped
salt
freshly ground black pepper

Cut the sole fillets in two lengthwise. Trim the salmon slices to the same size as the sole pieces (reserve any salmon trimmings). Place the salmon on top of the sole pieces and gently roll up the "sandwich." Secure with wooden toothpicks.

Bring the Court Bouillon to a boil in a deep skillet. Reduce the heat to a simmer and carefully add the rolled fillets. Simmer for 7 to 10 minutes, depending upon the thickness of the fish. Remove the fish with a slotted spoon and cool.

Peel and thinly slice the cucumber. Set aside.

Wash the cabbage leaves and set 4 aside. Cut the remaining 2 leaves into thin julienne strips.

Place the 4 red cabbage leaves on a large round platter. Place a rolled fillet on each leaf.

Toss together the julienned cabbage, sliced cucumber and reserved smoked salmon trimmings. Arrange the mixture in the center of the platter the rolled fillets. Sprinkle with the chopped chives and pine nuts.

In a food processor, place the bean curd, vinegar, shallot, salt and black pepper to taste. Process until the ingredients are puréed. Correct the seasoning and pour the sauce over the salad.

Eggs

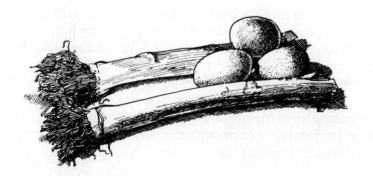

❦ Eggs with Cream ❦

Serves 4

W hen I was a child, we spent two weeks of our
vacation every year in a small town in Switzerland
with my mother's old nurse. She was an excellent
cook and on Sundays for lunch she used to make us eggs in
little white porcelain pots filled with cream. With the eggs
would be small sticks of toasted bread which she called
"mouillettes" (sippets). We would dunk them in the yolk and
eat the whites with a spoon. Whenever I think of our old
nurse, I remember the taste of those wonderful eggs and the
mouillettes melting in my mouth.

The eggs must be very fresh. Do not overcook them; the
yolks should be like a thick custard, and the whites opaque.

4 tablespoons unsalted
   butter, melted
4 extra-large eggs
4 tablespoons Crème
   Frâiche (see page 231)

salt
freshly ground pepper
4 teaspoons salmon caviar
16 Mouillettes (see the next
   recipe)

Preheat the oven to 325°F.

Pour 1 tablespoon of the melted butter into each of 4
5-ounce porcelain custard cups. Tilt the cups to butter the
sides.

Break 1 egg into each cup and sprinkle each with salt and
black pepper to taste. Place the cups in a baking pan and add
enough water to come halfway up the cups. Bake until the
eggs are nearly set, about 5 to 7 minutes. Place 1 tablespoon
of Crème Fraîche on top of each egg and bake for 2 to
3 minutes longer, or until the cream is hot.

Remove from the oven. Top each cup with a teaspoon of
salmon caviar. Place each cup on a plate, surround it with
Mouillettes and serve.

❦ Mouillettes ❦

Serves 4

6 large slices challah
2 tablespoons unsalted
   butter, softened

salt
freshly ground black pepper

Preheat the oven to 425°F.

Trim the crusts from the bread. Butter the slices and sprinkle them with salt and pepper to taste. Cut each slice into 5 or 6 strips and place them in a baking pan. Bake until golden brown.

❦ Poached Eggs ❦

Serves 4

*P*oached eggs are supposed to be easy to make, but I always had trouble with them. Mine looked disheveled, or they broke, or they turned into poached yolks that had no whites. I finally learned how to make beautiful poached eggs using this simple method.

2 quarts water
2 tablespoons wine vinegar

4 large eggs
vegetable oil

Place the water and vinegar in a large saucepan and bring to a boil. Reduce the heat to a simmer.

Lightly oil a ladle with some vegetable oil. Break an egg into the ladle and slowly lower the ladle into the water. Cook the egg for 4 minutes, or until the center of the yolk is cloudy.

Slide the egg from the ladle into a strainer to drain. The eggs may be gently rinsed under warm water to remove any trace of vinegar taste. Keep the egg warm while you repeat the process with the remaining eggs.

❧ Poached Eggs with ❧ Red and Green Sauce

Serves 4

W*hen serving this dish, first place a couple of tablespoons of the green sauce on the plate; then, carefully, pour next to it a couple of tablespoons of the red sauce. In between them, place the poached eggs.*

2 cups Tomato Coulis (see page 236)
4 Poached Eggs (see page 87)
salt
freshly ground black pepper

2 cups Pesto (see page 241)
2 cups Fried Onion Rings (see page 213)
2 tablespoons chopped chives

Spoon enough Tomato Coulis onto 4 individual serving plates to cover the bottoms. Place a Poached Egg on top of each plate. Sprinkle with salt and pepper to taste. Cover half of each egg with some of the Pesto sauce. Garnish each plate with Fried Onion Rings and sprinkle the uncovered half of each egg with some of the chives. Serve immediately.

Fried Eggs and Eggplant

Serves 4

1 eggplant, about ¾ pound, trimmed
salt
4 tablespoons all-purpose flour

about ⅓ cup vegetable oil
4 large eggs
freshly ground black pepper
1 tablespoon chopped parsley

Cut the eggplant lengthwise into 4 slices. With the tip of a sharp knife, score diagonal lines across each slice without cutting through; then score diagonal lines the opposite direction to form a diamond pattern on each slice. Sprinkle the slices with salt and set them aside for 10 minutes to let the salt draw out water. Pat the eggplant slices dry with paper towels.

Dust the eggplant slices with the flour.

In a large skillet, heat ¼ cup of the oil over medium-high heat. Add the eggplant slices and fry them for 1 minute on each side, adding more oil if necessary. Remove the slices to an ovenproof platter lined with paper towels and keep them warm in a very low oven (200°F).

Rinse and dry the skillet, then add 1 tablespoon of oil and heat it. Break the eggs into the skillet and fry them to the desired doneness.

Place a slice of eggplant on each of 4 individual serving plates. Top each slice with a fried egg. Season with black pepper to taste and sprinkle with the chopped parsley. Serve immediately.

⚗ Omelet Stuffed with ⚗ Zucchini and Spinach

Serves 4

2 tablespoons unsalted
    butter
4 small zucchini, diced
½ pound fresh spinach,
    stemmed and chopped
salt

freshly ground black pepper
1 tablespoon chopped fresh
    thyme or 1 teaspoon
    dried thyme
6 large eggs, lightly beaten

In a large skillet, melt the butter over medium-high heat. Add the zucchini and sauté for 3 minutes, stirring with a wooden spoon. Add the spinach and sprinkle with salt and black pepper to taste. Sauté for 1 minute more.

Pour the beaten eggs over the zucchini and spinach and reduce the heat to medium. With a fork, pull the edges of the omelet toward the center as they begin to set, tilting the skillet so that the uncooked portion of the eggs runs over the cooked edges. With a fork, push the center back toward the edges.

When the omelet is nearly set, sprinkle it with the thyme. With a spatula, fold the omelet over and cook for 1 minute more. Slide the omelet onto a platter and serve immediately.

Omelet Stuffed with Chicken Livers

Serves 4

1 pound chicken livers
4 tablespoons vegetable oil
1 teaspoon dried tarragon
salt
freshly ground black pepper
2 slices white bread

¼ cup Chicken Stock (see page 49)
6 large eggs, lightly beaten
watercress sprigs, for garnish

Trim the livers, removing any gristle and fat.

In a large skillet, heat 2 tablespoons of the oil over medium heat. Add the chicken livers and sauté lightly for 2 to 3 minutes on each side. Sprinkle with the tarragon and salt and black pepper to taste. Set aside to cool.

In a small bowl, soak the bread in the Chicken Stock. Squeeze the liquid from the bread.

Place the chicken livers and the bread in a food processor. Purée and set the mixture aside.

In a large skillet, heat the remaining oil over high heat. Pour in the beaten eggs and reduce the heat to medium. With a fork, pull the edges of the omelet toward the center as they begin to set, tilting the skillet so that the uncooked portion of the eggs runs under the cooked edges. With a fork, push the center back toward the edges.

When the eggs are nearly set, spread the liver purée over them. With a spatula, fold the omelet over, enclosing the purée. Cook for 1 minute more. Turn off the heat and slide the omelet onto a platter. Garnish with watercress sprigs.

❧ Omelette Provençale ❧

Serves 6

Years ago, *when I first came to this country, I tried to please my mother-in-law by making what I thought was a Western omelet, using lots of ketchup. It was a disaster! After the first ketchup omelet, my mother-in-law called me to her room and said in a rather mocking tone that she would cook American and I should keep to French cooking. My Western omelet, she added, was so awful that not even her cat would eat it! I went back to cooking French.*

This is my mother's favorite omelet recipe. It is a meal in itself; so serve it with a good bread, a green salad and a cool bottle of dry white wine for a hot summer lunch. The ingredients below do not call for salt, as anchovies are quite salty.

4 tablespoons extra-virgin olive oil
2 onions, thinly chopped
1 green pepper, diced
1 sweet red pepper, diced
3 tomatoes, peeled, quartered, seeded and sliced
2 tablespoons chopped chives or basil

freshly ground black pepper
12 large eggs
1 tablespoon unsalted butter
12 anchovy fillets, drained but ¼ teaspoon of their oil reserved
watercress sprigs, for garnish

In a large skillet (if using a smaller skillet, halve the recipe and make it in two batches), heat 2 tablespoons of the olive oil over medium heat. Add the onions, green pepper and sweet red peppers and sauté until the onions are transparent. With a slotted spoon, remove the onions and peppers to a plate.

Add another tablespoon of the olive oil to the skillet and heat. Add the tomatoes and sauté them over medium heat, stirring often, for 10 minutes. Sprinkle with the chopped chives or basil and the black pepper to taste. With a slotted spoon, remove the tomatoes to a plate.

In a large mixing bowl, beat the eggs with a wire whisk.

Rinse and dry the skillet, add the remaining olive oil and the butter and heat over medium heat until the butter sizzles. Add the eggs all at once. With a fork, pull the edges of the omelet toward the center as they begin to set, tilting the skillet so that the uncooked portion of the eggs runs over the cooked edges. When the eggs are half set, spread the onions and peppers in the center of the omelet. Surround them with the tomatoes, place the anchovy fillets on top and drizzle with the anchovy oil. With a spatula, fold the omelet over the filling and cook for 1 minute longer.

Slide the omelet onto a serving platter. Garnish with the watercress sprigs and serve immediately.

🐛 Omelet with Smoked 🐛
Mozzarella and Basil

Serves 6

My street in New York City used to be Italian, but today it has attracted people from all over and very few vestiges of the old neighborhood remain. However, we still have the best dairy store in the city. Grace, the owner, and her son make a superb smoked mozzarella which inspired this recipe.

It is important to use fresh smoked mozzarella, because the soft cheese will quickly melt into the eggs. If you are using supermarket mozzarella, cut it in thin slices so as to obtain the same results.

Serve the omelet with toasted bialys.

20 large fresh basil leaves
10 large eggs
salt
freshly ground black pepper
½ pound smoked
    mozzarella, sliced

5 tablespoons unsalted
    butter
watercress sprigs, for
    garnish

Wash and dry the basil leaves, then chop them finely.

Break the eggs into a large bowl. Add the basil and salt and black pepper to taste and beat with a fork.

In a large skillet, heat the butter over medium-high heat. When it foams, add the egg mixture all at once. With a fork, pull the edges of the omelet toward the center as they begin to set, tilting the skillet so that the uncooked portion of the eggs runs over the cooked edges. With a fork, push the center back toward the edges.

Spread the mozzarella slices over the omelet and cook for 5 minutes longer, or until the cheese starts to melt.

With a spatula, fold the omelet over the cheese and cook for 2 to 3 minutes more. Slide the omelet onto a hot serving platter and garnish with the watercress sprigs.

🥚 Matzo Brei 🥚

Serves 4

I soak the matzo overnight in the beaten eggs and then fry it as a pancake. This results in a texture closer to that of the French pain perdu—*more like a cake than like scrambled eggs.*

3 large eggs	powdered sugar
3 tablespoons heavy cream	ground cinnamon
3 matzos	maple syrup
¼ cup vegetable oil for frying	

In a large mixing bowl, beat the eggs with the cream.

Break the matzos into bite-sized pieces and add them to the bowl. Mix well. Let stand at room temperature overnight.

In a large skillet, heat the oil over medium-high heat. When the oil is hot, add the matzo brei mixture and cook for 3 to 4 minutes, or until the bottom is golden brown. With a spatula, turn the pancake over. Cook for 4 minutes longer.

Drain on a paper towel and cut into wedges. Serve sprinkled with powdered sugar mixed with cinnamon, or with maple syrup.

Fish

Salmon en Papillote with Mustard Sauce

Serves 4

In French, en papillote *means wrapped in paper. Here each salmon steak is wrapped in waxed paper and then steamed. This method is excellent for any fish, because the paper seals in the natural flavors and juices of the fish.*

4 ounces wakame (dried
    Japanese seaweed)
4 salmon steaks, about
    1 inch thick
4 scallions, trimmed and cut
    into 2-inch pieces
2 rosemary sprigs, cut in
    half, or ½ teaspoon
    dried rosemary

salt
freshly ground black pepper
4 ounces sliced pickled
    ginger
2 lemons, cut into wedges
1 cup Mustard Sauce (see
    page 239)

Cut four 12-inch squares of waxed paper.

Soak the wakame in a large bowl of cold water to cover for 4 minutes. Drain and cut it into pieces 5 inches long.

Place some wakame on each waxed-paper square. Top with a salmon steak, pieces of scallion and a half a rosemary sprig. Sprinkle with salt and black pepper to taste. Fold the waxed paper securely around the salmon.

Place the salmon packages in a bamboo or metal steamer and steam for 8 minutes.

Place a salmon package on each individual serving plate. With scissors, cut out a 3-inch square opening in the waxed paper. Place a lemon wedge and a few slices of pickled ginger in each opening and serve with Mustard Sauce.

Chopped Raw Tuna with Ginger Sauce

Serves 6

O n a trip to Japan I was served a wonderful dish of chopped raw tuna on a bed of seaweed with fresh horseradish sauce. Back in the United States, I tried to reproduce this recipe. Unable to find fresh Japanese horseradish, I served the tuna with my own Ginger Sauce (see page 239); you could also use a mayonnaise or sour cream sauce. This dish is excellent as an appetizer or as a main course for lunch on a hot summer day. Prepare the tuna the night before to let it marinate in the lime juice overnight.

2 pounds fresh tuna
½ cup lime juice
1 tablespoon chopped chives
1 tablespoon chopped parsley
1 tablespoon chopped dill
4 shallots, chopped
salt
freshly ground black pepper
1 head Boston lettuce, leaves separated
2 sweet red peppers, sliced into rings and seeded
½ cup Ginger Sauce (see page 239)

Remove the skin and bones from the tuna (or ask the fishmonger to do it for you). Cut the fish into 1-inch strips; then cut each strip into ½-inch cubes. With a sharp knife, coarsely chop the cubes.

In a mixing bowl, place the chopped fish and add the lime juice, chives, parsley, dill and chopped shallots. Sprinkle with salt and black pepper to taste. Mix well, cover, and refrigerate overnight.

Line each individual serving plate with one or two lettuce leaves. Place some chopped tuna in the center. Decorate with red pepper rings. Serve with Ginger Sauce on the side.

Fillet of Sole with Green Bananas

Serves 6

I lived for several months in East Africa, where very often we were served stews with sliced green bananas. They were delicious, tasting more like a sweet potato than a banana. Back in the United States, I started to experiment with these bananas. They are found everywhere, in supermarkets and fruit and vegetable stores. Choose bananas that are firm but not too hard, or they will take longer to cook.

12 sole or flounder fillets, about 3 pounds

salt

freshly ground black pepper

3 tablespoons all-purpose flour

3 tablespoons olive oil

3 medium onions, sliced

6 green bananas, peeled and sliced

3 tablespoons unsalted butter

1½ tablespoons red wine vinegar

12 mint leaves, for garnish

3 lemons, cut in wedges

Sprinkle the fish with salt and black pepper to taste. Place the flour on a plate and roll the fillets in it. Shake off any excess flour. Set the fish aside.

In a large skillet, heat 2 tablespoons of the olive oil over high heat. Add the onions, reduce the heat to medium and cook for 3 minutes. Add the sliced bananas, sprinkle with salt and black pepper and cook for 12 minutes more, carefully turning the bananas with a spatula from time to time, until the bananas are golden brown. Remove from the heat and keep warm.

In another skillet, heat the remaining oil with the butter over medium heat. When the butter is hot, add the fish and

cook for 4 minutes. Turn the fillets and cook for another
4 minutes. Add the wine vinegar, pouring it in around the
edges of the skillet. Cook for 30 seconds more and remove
from the heat.

Transfer the fish to a large serving platter. Surround with
the sliced bananas and onions. Garnish with the mint leaves
and serve with lemon wedges.

❧ Swiss Chard Stuffed ❧ with Fish

Serves 6

*This intriguing dish can be served hot or it can be made
in advance, refrigerated and served cold. In either case,
it should be served with Horseradish Sauce (see
page 238). When shopping for this dish, choose large leaves
of chard and count on about two leaves per person. The
stems become part of the stuffing.*

2 pounds (about 12 large
   leaves) Swiss chard
8 cups boiling water
1 small head Boston lettuce
2 pounds whitefish fillets,
   cut into 1-inch pieces
2 eggs, lightly beaten
2 tablespoons chopped fresh
   thyme or 1½ teaspoons
   dried thyme

2 tablespoons drained small
   capers
2 tablespoons grated lime
   peel
1 tablespoon black sesame
   seeds
salt
freshly ground black pepper
2 cups Horseradish Sauce
   (see page 238)

101

Rinse the Swiss chard well. Cut off and reserve the stems. Place the leaves in a large colander and slowly pour the boiling water over them. Rinse well under cold water and drain. Pat the leaves dry with paper towels and set aside. Break the Boston lettuce into leaves and rinse well. Drain and set aside.

Put the reserved Swiss chard stems, fish fillets and eggs in a food processor. Process just until the ingredients are finely chopped. Pour the mixture into a large mixing bowl and add the thyme, capers, grated lime peel, sesame seeds, and salt and black pepper to taste. Mix well.

Spread the reserved Swiss chard leaves out on a work surface. Place 2 heaping tablespoonfuls of the fish mixture on the edge of a leaf. Roll the leaf up tightly, tucking in the ends to form a neat package. Repeat with the remaining leaves.

Line the basket of a bamboo or metal steamer with the reserved Boston lettuce leaves. Place the stuffed Swiss chard packages in the basket, seam-sides down. Half-fill the lower part of the steamer with boiling water, place the basket on top, cover and steam for 8 minutes.

If a bamboo steamer is used, serve the stuffed leaves from the steamer basket, with the Horseradish Sauce in a separate dish. If a metal steamer is used, arrange the leaves in a circle on a serving platter, leaving an opening in the center to be filled with a dish of Horseradish Sauce.

Sardines des Pyrénées
ᕰ (Deep-Fried Sardines ᕰ with Black Olives)

Serves 4

I first had this dish in the Pyrénées mountains of Spain. Fresh sardines are available in this country. However, if you cannot find them, use large smelts instead. Ask the fishmonger to remove the center bone and cut off the head. He may complain, but maybe if you smile and speak to him about Spain, he will do it for you.

12 fresh sardines or smelts, center bones and heads removed

salt

freshly ground black pepper

2 eggs, beaten

1 cup fine unflavored breadcrumbs

vegetable oil for deep frying

½ pound black Nice olives

2 lemons, cut in wedges

1 small bunch parsley, for garnish

kosher salt

Wash the fish and pat them dry with paper towels. Rub the fish inside and out with salt and black pepper. Spread the fish open.

Dip the fish in the beaten eggs and then roll them in the breadcrumbs. Set aside.

Heat the oil in a deep fryer or deep heavy skillet until it reaches 360°F on a deep-frying thermometer. Fry the fish until they are golden brown. Drain on paper towels.

Place the parsley in the center of a large platter and arrange the fried fish all around it. Place some olives on top of each fish. Place the lemon wedges on the platter and garnish with parsley. Serve with a bowl of kosher salt. Guests should sprinkle some salt and squeeze a drop of lemon juice on their fish.

103

🦪 Broiled Fresh Herrings 🦪 Stuffed with Fennel

Serves 4

*A*sk the fishmonger to remove the center bone of the fish, leaving on the heads and tails. If herring is unavailable, use smelt.

1 fennel bulb
4 fresh herrings or 8 smelts
2 tablespoons softened
   unsalted butter
salt

freshly ground black pepper
1 4-ounce jar pickled vine
   leaves, drained
2 tablespoons olive oil
2 lemons, cut into wedges

Preheat the broiler.

Trim the fennel bulb and set aside some of the leaves for a garnish. Quarter the bulb. Using the fine julienne blade of a food processor, julienne the fennel.

Make 2 deep cuts in the belly of each fish. Rub some butter inside the fish cavities. Fill the cavities with the julienned fennel. Sprinkle the fish, inside and out, with salt and black pepper and set aside.

Rinse the vine leaves to remove some of the salt. Pat them dry with paper towels.

Spread 4 to 5 vine leaves on a work surface, with each leaf overlapping the next one. Place a fish on top of the leaves and roll up the leaves, enclosing the fish. Tie the package closed with kitchen string. Repeat with the remaining leaves and herrings. Brush each package with olive oil. Arrange them on a broiling pan and broil for 4 minutes on each side.

Remove the fish to a platter. Cut off the strings. Garnish with the reserved fennel leaves and serve with lemon wedges.

Baked Tile Fish with Star Fruit

Serves 4

*S*tar fruit, or carambola, is a beautiful yellow fruit about six inches long with four to six strong longitudinal ribs; when sliced, the fruit has the shape of a star. There are two types of star fruit: a sweet variety, used in pies and preserves or eaten fresh in fruit salad, and a slightly sour one for savory dishes. In this dish I use the slightly sour carambolas to counterbalance the sweetness of the fish.

4 thick tile fish steaks
salt
freshly ground black pepper
½ cup water
2 tablespoons dark soy
   sauce or low-sodium
   soy sauce

¼ teaspoon sesame oil
2 star fruit, thinly sliced
2 tablespoons chopped
   parsley
2 lemons, cut into wedges

Preheat the oven to 400°F.

Wipe the fish steaks with paper towels and arrange them in a baking dish. Sprinkle with salt and black pepper to taste.

In a bowl, mix together the water, soy sauce and sesame oil. Pour over the fish and bake for 8 minutes. Scatter the star fruit slices over the fish and bake for 6 minutes more.

Remove the fish to a serving platter. Arrange the sliced star fruit on and around the fish, pour some of the sauce over the fish, sprinkle with the chopped parsley and serve with lemon wedges.

Red Mullet with Basil and Tomatoes

Serves 6

This dish should be served at room temperature, garnished with lemon wedges. It can be made with red snapper or a small salmon instead. Saffron is the dried bright orange stamen of the saffron crocus. Real saffron is expensive; however, you only need 3 or 4 stamens. Soak the stamens in a tablespoon of cold water for 10 minutes before adding them (water and stamens) to the saucepan.

6 small red mullets, about
　½ pound each
3 cups water
2 tablespoons olive oil
2 large tomatoes, about
　1 pound
⅔ cup dry white wine
1 small onion, thinly sliced
16 medium-sized fresh basil
　leaves

1 garlic clove
10 whole coriander seeds
⅛ teaspoon saffron, soaked
　in 1 tablespoon cold
　water
½ teaspoon salt
freshly ground white pepper
1 tablespoon chopped fresh
　parsley
2 lemons, cut into wedges

Preheat the oven to 475°F.

Wash the fish and pat dry. Oil a baking dish large enough to hold all the fish side by side. Place the fish in the baking dish and brush on some olive oil. Set aside while preparing the tomatoes.

In a medium saucepan, bring 3 cups of water to a boil. Add the tomatoes, turn off the heat and let the tomatoes stand in the hot water for 4 minutes. Drain and rinse the tomatoes under cold running water. Peel, halve and seed the tomatoes; then cut them into small dice.

In a medium saucepan, place the white wine, diced tomatoes, onion, 10 basil leaves, coriander, garlic, saffron and soaking liquid, and salt and white pepper to taste. Bring to a boil, reduce the heat, and simmer, covered, for 10 minutes.

Pour the sauce over the fish. Seal the baking dish with foil and bake for 5 minutes.

Remove the baking dish from the oven. Uncover the dish, place a fresh basil leaf on each fish and let the fish cool to room temperature. (If the fish is to be served the next day, do not remove the foil. Refrigerate; remove from the refrigerator at least 2 hours before serving, and place the basil leaves on the fish just before serving.) Sprinkle the chopped parsley over the fish and serve from the baking dish, with the lemon wedges.

❦ Trout with Olives ❦

Serves 4

One of the few fish that are still excellent even when frozen are river trout from Idaho. They often come without the center bone. If you buy fresh trout, ask the fishmonger to remove the center bone but leave the heads and the tails. This recipe can also be made with any individual whole fish.

Serve the trout with boiled new potatoes.

4 boned trout
1 lemon, quartered
salt
freshly ground black pepper
5 tablespoons unsalted
    butter
2 tablespoons olive oil
½ pound Greek olives,
    pitted and chopped
2 tablespoons chopped fresh
    thyme or 2 teaspoons
    dried thyme
4 tablespoons drained
    capers
1 4-ounce can pitted black
    olives, sliced
6 tablespoons lemon juice
4 tablespoons chopped fresh
    parsley

Preheat the oven to 450°F.

Rub the fish inside and out with the lemon quarters; discard the lemon. Sprinkle with salt and black pepper and set aside.

In an ovenproof dish, melt 2 tablespoons of the butter with the olive oil. Add half the chopped Greek olives and the thyme. Mix well and remove from the heat.

Roll the fish in the butter-oil mixture and arrange them side by side in the dish. Bake for 20 minutes, basting the fish from time to time with the pan juices.

In a medium skillet, melt the remaining butter over medium heat. Cook the butter until it is light brown. Add the capers, the sliced olives and the remaining chopped olives. Add the lemon juice, mix well, and remove from the heat.

Arrange the fish on a serving platter. Pour the olive butter over them and sprinkle with the chopped parsley. Serve immediately.

Tile Fish Steaks with Spinach

Serves 4

Serve this dish with Rice Noodles (see page 225) and the mushroom sauce from the recipe for Seme di Melone (see page 228).

2 pounds fresh spinach
1 lemon
1 cup water
4 tile fish steaks
4 tablespoons unsalted
  butter
2 shallots, chopped
¾ cup dry white wine
2 tablespoons chopped
  parsley

1 tablespoon chopped fresh
  thyme or 1 teaspoon
  dried thyme
salt
freshly ground black pepper
6 tablespoons lemon juice
½ cup plain yogurt
3 tablespoons Crème
  Fraîche (see page 000) or
  sour cream

Trim the stems and any discolored or blemished leaves from the spinach. Wash thoroughly and drain. Set aside.

Peel the lemon and julienne the zest. Thinly slice the peeled lemon.

In a small saucepan, bring the water to a boil. Add the lemon zest and bring back to a boil. Remove from the heat and strain off the liquid. Set the cooked zest aside.

Place the tile fish steaks in a bamboo or metal steamer and steam for 10 minutes over boiling water. Set aside and keep warm.

To prepare the sauce, in a medium skillet melt 2 tablespoons of the butter over medium heat. Add the shallots, reduce the heat and sauté gently until transparent.

Add the white wine, parsley, thyme and salt and black pepper to taste. Stir and cook over high heat until the liquid is reduced by half. Add the lemon juice and the zest and cook for 1 minute.

In a small bowl, mix the Crème Fraîche with the yogurt. Add to the sauce, stirring constantly. Gently cook the sauce over very low heat just until it is heated through; do not let it boil. Turn off the heat.

Spread the spinach leaves on an oval serving platter. Dot them with the remaining butter and sprinkle with salt and black pepper. Place the fish steaks on top of the spinach and lightly sprinkle them with salt and black pepper. Pour half the sauce over the fish. Garnish with the lemon slices. Serve the remaining sauce in a sauceboat.

Potato and Herring Pie

Serves 6

I was once taken to a kosher supermarket in Brooklyn by my friend Toby, whose stories about her childhood and her mother's cooking made my mouth water. As we stood next to the deli counter wondering what to buy for lunch, she told me of a recipe her grandmother used to make. Toby loved it but could only say it was made with "schmaltz herring, potatoes and I don't know what else." I bought schmaltz herring and potatoes and invented the "what else"! Toby says the pie is wonderful—as good as her grandmother's.

110

When buying the herring, be sure to ask for extra onions and ask the counterperson to cut the herring into very small pieces. This recipe could be served as an appetizer, or as a main course for lunch. If you are serving it as an appetizer, make it in small, individual porcelain soufflé dishes, about 4-ounce capacity. As a main course, use any 1 1/2-quart au gratin dish—glass, metal or porcelain.

3 pounds Idaho potatoes, peeled and quartered

2 schmaltz herring fillets, cut into 1/2-inch pieces

2 tablespoons sliced onions (from the herring)

1 egg

1/4 cup milk

3 tablespoons unsalted butter

1/2 cup grated Swiss cheese

freshly ground black pepper

salt

1/4 pound sliced Swiss cheese

2 sprigs fresh thyme or 1/4 teaspoon dried thyme

Place the potatoes in a large saucepan, cover them with cold water and bring to a boil. Lower the heat to medium and cook for 25 minutes or until the potatoes are soft when pierced with a fork.

Drain the potatoes and push them through a fine sieve placed over a large bowl. (This can be done easily using the back of a wooden spoon. It is important never to use a food processor; the purée will become very gummy.)

Preheat the oven to 475°F.

Add to the purée the herring, onions, egg, milk and 2 tablespoons of the butter. Mix well. Add the grated cheese and the black pepper. Taste the purée before adding salt; schmaltz herrings are very salty.

Fill the soufflé dishes or au gratin dish with the purée. Sprinkle thyme on top. Cover the thyme with the sliced Swiss cheese. Dot with the remaining butter and bake until the cheese is melted and golden brown. Serve immediately.

Flounder with Bean Sprouts

Serves 4

*B*ean sprouts are available in all supermarkets and fruit
and vegetable stores. Loose, fresh bean sprouts are the
best—brown tips mean the sprouts are old. Any firm
white fish fillet can be used in this recipe.

4 to 6 flounder fillets, about
    2 pounds
4 tablespoons all-purpose
    flour
3 tablespoons butter
2 tablespoons olive oil
3 leeks, white parts only

½ pound bean sprouts
1 tablespoon raspberry or
    red wine vinegar
1 tablespoon drained capers
salt
freshly ground black pepper
1 tablespoon chopped dill

Wash the flounder fillets and pat them dry with paper towels.
Dust each fillet with flour and set aside.

In a large skillet, heat the butter and the olive oil over
high heat. When the butter foams, add the fish and cook for
3 minutes. Turn the fillets and cook for 5 to 6 minutes
longer. Remove the fish to a serving platter and keep warm in
a 200°F oven.

Wash the leeks thoroughly and cut them in two
lengthwise. Thinly julienne each half.

Add the leeks to the skillet used for the fish. Cook them
over medium heat, stirring constantly, until transparent,
about 8 minutes. Add the bean sprouts and cook for 1 minute,
stirring constantly until the leeks and bean sprouts are well
mixed. Remove the skillet from the heat; add the vinegar and
capers. Mix well. Add salt and black pepper to taste. Pour
the sauce over the fish. Sprinkle with the dill and serve.

Cold Mackerel with Cucumber

Serves 6

1 long Japanese cucumber
3 cups Fish Stock (see
  page 48)
2 onions, sliced
1 carrot, sliced
1 bay leaf
6 small whole mackerel,
  cleaned

1 cup Crème Fraîche (see
  page 231) or plain
  yogurt
2 tablespoons lemon juice
salt
freshly ground black pepper
2 tablespoons chopped
  parsley

Peel the cucumber lengthwise, leaving several ¼-inch strips
of skin. Slice the cucumber very thinly. Place the cucumber
slices in a large bowl and cover with iced water. Let stand for
2 hours.

Preheat the oven to 375°F.

In a saucepan, place the Fish Stock, onions, carrots and
bay leaf. Bring to a boil, reduce the heat and cook for
10 minutes.

Place the mackerel side by side in a baking pan. Pour 2
cups of the Fish Stock over them, cover with aluminum foil
and bake for 8 minutes. Remove from the oven and cool.

When the mackerel are cold, carefully lift them with two
spatulas and place them on a large serving platter. (Mackerel
are fragile and break easily.) Garnish with slices of the
cooked carrots and onions. Refrigerate until ready to serve.

Just before serving, beat the Crème Fraîche or yogurt
with the lemon juice and salt and black pepper.

Drain the cucumbers and pat them dry with paper
towels. Place the cucumbers in a large bowl, add the Crème
Fraîche or yogurt and toss the salad. Arrange the cucumber
salad around the fish. Sprinkle with chopped parsley and
serve.

🍂 Stuffed Whole Salmon 🍂

Serves 8

F or this very festive dish, you will need a large roasting pan and a long, oval serving platter. When buying the salmon, ask the fishmonger to leave the head and the tail but to remove the center bone. The fish gets an unusual, delicious flavor from wakame leaves, a type of Japanese seaweed available in Oriental groceries and health-food stores. Serve with Garlic Butter (see page 233) and fresh spinach noodles.

6 tablespoons unsalted
   butter
3 carrots, julienned
3 celery stalks, julienned
2 onions, julienned
2 medium cucumbers,
   peeled and julienned
3 shallots, chopped
1 teaspoon dried thyme
salt
freshly ground black pepper
¼ pound white mushrooms

1 whole salmon, about 6 to
   7½ pounds
1 3-inch piece fresh ginger
   root, peeled and
   julienned
1 ounce dry wakame
   seaweed, soaked in cold
   water for 5 minutes
2 cups water
1 cup dry white wine
1 bunch parsley, for garnish
1 cup Garlic Butter (see
   page 233)

Preheat the oven to 375°F.

In a large saucepan, melt 3 tablespoons of the butter over medium-high heat. Add the julienned vegetables, shallots, thyme and salt and black pepper to taste. Lower the heat, cover and simmer for 10 minutes, stirring occasionally; do not let the vegetables brown. Set aside.

Wash the mushrooms; pat them dry and remove the stems (save the stems for another use). With a knife, julienne the mushrooms (do not use a food processor; mushrooms break easily).

In a skillet, melt the remaining butter over medium-high heat; add the mushrooms and sauté for 3 minutes. Sprinkle with salt and black pepper to taste. Remove the mushrooms with a slotted spoon and add them to the vegetables.

Sprinkle the surface and cavity of the salmon with salt and black pepper. Sprinkle the cavity with the julienned ginger. Stuff the cavity with the julienned vegetables. Close the cavity with wooden toothpicks.

Drain the wakame. Line a roasting pan with half the wakame and place the salmon on top. Cover the fish with the remaining wakame. Add the water and white wine to the pan. Cover the pan with aluminum foil and bake for 1 hour, basting with the pan juices from time to time. Add more wine and water, in equal proportions, if necessary.

With two spatulas, carefully remove the fish to a long serving platter. Discard the seaweed. With a sharp knife, make a shallow horizontal incision near the head and another one near the tail. Peel off the salmon skin. Dip the parsley sprigs in the pan juices and garnish the fish with them.

Strain the pan juices through a fine sieve placed over a bowl. Serve the fish with the pan juices and the Garlic Butter on the side.

Deep-Fried Flounder
❦ with Horseradish ❦
Sauce

Serves 4

*T*he flounders for this recipe should be no larger than
¾ pound each. Flounders this size are easy to find in
the summer, especially if you are vacationing near the
sea. Serve 1 fish per person with grated daikon and
Horseradish Sauce (see page 238).

4 small whole flounders,
    about ¾ pound each
½ cup all-purpose flour
salt
freshly ground black pepper
vegetable oil for deep frying

1 whole daikon, peeled and
    grated
½ cup pickled sliced ginger,
    drained
Horseradish Sauce (see
    page 238)
kosher salt

Wash the flounders and pat them dry with paper towels.
    In a shallow bowl, mix the flour with salt and black
pepper. Roll the flounders in the flour, then shake them to
remove any excess. Set aside.
    Heat the oil in a deep fryer or deep heavy skillet until it
reaches 360°F on a deep-frying thermometer. Fry the
flounders, one by one, until they are golden brown. Drain
each fish on a platter lined with paper towels, then place it in
a 300°F oven to keep warm while you continue frying the
other fish.
    When ready to serve, arrange each fish on an individual
plate. Next to the flounder's mouth place a small mound of
grated daikon and 2 or 3 slices of pickled ginger. Serve with
Horseradish Sauce and kosher salt.

Baked Mackerel in Wine

Serves 6

6 medium mackerels, cleaned
salt
freshly ground black pepper
3 leeks, white part only
4 tablespoons unsalted
    butter or margarine

3 onions, chopped
1 cup dry white wine
2 lemons, sliced
¼ cup Crème Fraîche (see
    page 231)
2 teaspoons strong Dijon
    mustard

Preheat the oven to 400°F.

Rinse the mackerels and pat dry with paper towels. Sprinkle with salt and black pepper and set aside.

Wash the leeks thoroughly and cut them in two lengthwise. Thinly julienne each half.

In a skillet, melt 2 tablespoons of the butter or margarine over medium heat. Add the onions and leeks and cook until they are transparent but not brown. Add salt and black pepper to taste and the white wine. Bring to a boil, then turn off the heat.

Lightly grease a large baking pan. With a slotted spoon, remove the onions and leeks from the skillet and place them in the bottom of the baking pan. Arrange the lemon slices in a layer on top. Place the mackerels on top of the lemons. Pour the liquid from the skillet over the fish. Dot the fish with the remaining butter or margarine. Bake for 25 minutes.

With a spatula, remove the fish to a serving platter. Place a cooked slice of lemon on each fish.

Strain the pan liquids through a fine sieve into a saucepan.

In a bowl beat together the Crème Fraîche and the mustard. Pour the mixture into the strained pan juices, stirring constantly. Cook gently over very low heat just until the sauce is heated through; do not let the sauce boil. Pour the sauce into a sauceboat and serve with the fish.

❧ Shad Roe with ❧ Cardoons

Serves 4

Cardoons, *which look like overgrown celery, are delicious if you cook only the tender stalks. The French use them with beef marrow, but this recipe with shad roe is more fun and easier to make. The edges of the stalks are very prickly; so be careful how you handle them.*

1 medium-size cardoon, about 1½ pounds
2 tablespoons all-purpose flour
4½ cups water
3 tablespoons lemon juice
4 fresh shad roe portions
4 tablespoons unsalted butter

1 tablespoon chopped fresh dill
salt
freshly ground black pepper
1 lemon, thinly sliced, for garnish
parsley sprigs, for garnish

Remove and discard the tough stalks of the cardoon. Carefully peel the stringy part of the remaining stalks as you would celery, keeping only the center of the stalks. Cut each stalk into 3-inch pieces.

In a bowl, mix the flour with ½ cup of the water.

In a large saucepan, bring the remaining water to a boil. Add the flour-and-water mixture and 1½ tablespoons of the lemon juice. Add the cardoon pieces and bring to a boil. Simmer for 35 minutes or until the cardoons are easily pierced with a fork.

Meanwhile, remove the veins and any loose membranes from the shad roe. In a large skillet, melt the butter over medium heat. Add the shad roe and cook gently for

8 minutes; carefully turn them over and cook for 8 minutes longer.

Drain the cardoons well and arrange them on a platter. Sprinkle with the dill and salt and black pepper to taste. Top with the shad roe.

Add the remaining lemon juice to the skillet and cook for 1 minute over medium heat, scraping the sides of the skillet. Pour the pan juices over the roe. Garnish with lemon slices and parsley sprigs and serve.

Cold Stuffed Carp in Aspic

Serves 6

*T*he carp's head stands at one end of the platter surrounded by the stuffed slices, which form the body of the fish. This dish can be served hot, but it is spectacular cold.

1 5-pound carp, cleaned
3 quarts water
2 pounds fish heads and
    bones
2 carrots, cut into 2-inch
    pieces
2 celery stalks, cut into
    1-inch pieces
1 large onion, stuck with
    1 clove
1 bay leaf
2 pounds whitefish fillets,
    cut into 2-inch pieces

3 egg yolks
2 tablespoons chopped
    parsley
⅛ teaspoon ground cumin
salt
freshly ground black pepper
4 egg whites
2 carrots, thinly sliced
watercress sprigs, for
    garnish
lemon wedges, for garnish
Horseradish Sauce (see
    page 238)

119

Ask the fishmonger to cut off the carp's head vertically so that the head will stand up easily; the body of the fish should be cut vertically into 1¼-inch slices.

In a large pot, bring the water to a boil. Add the carp head and the fish bones and heads, the thick carrot pieces, the celery stalks, the onion and the bay leaf. Bring to a boil, reduce the heat and simmer for 20 minutes, skimming the surface often.

With a sharp-pointed knife, remove the skin from the carp slices, being careful not to tear the skin. Set the skins aside. Remove the bones from the fish and place all the fish in a food processor. Add the whitefish fillets, egg yolks, parsley, cumin and salt and black pepper to taste. Process until the mixture is a smooth paste.

In a large bowl, beat the egg whites with a pinch of salt until they are stiff. Fold the fish mixture into the egg whites. Correct the seasoning.

With a spoon, fill the reserved fish skins with the fish mixture to form slices. Set aside.

Remove the carp head from the fish stock and set aside. Strain the fish stock through a fine colander into a large saucepan. Add the thin carrot slices, bring the stock to a boil and reduce the heat to a simmer. Add the stuffed fish slices and poach for 8 minutes.

With a spatula, carefully remove the fish slices to an oval platter. Place the reserved carp head at one end and arrange the poached slices, overlapping, to form the fish's body. Place a thin slice of carrot on top of each fish slice.

Strain the fish stock again and pour it over the fish. Serve warm or refrigerate until chilled.

Garnish the fish with watercress sprigs and lemon wedges. Serve Horseradish Sauce on the side.

❦ Bluefish with Kohlrabi ❦

Serves 4

*T*his is a cold dish for hot evenings in the summer, when the bluefish is at its best. Kohlrabi is a strange vegetable that looks as if it had been invented by a mad scientist —round, light green, about the size of a potato, with "tentacles" all around (which are, in reality, its root system).

2 pounds kohlrabi
salt
freshly ground black pepper
½ cup Anchovy Vinaigrette
    (see page 230)
4 cups water
1 cup dry white wine
1 onion, stuck with 2 cloves

1 bay leaf
2 pounds bluefish fillets
2 cups Mayonnaise (see
    page 240)
2 limes, thinly sliced, for
    garnish
2 tablespoons chopped fresh
    dill, for garnish

Peel the kohlrabi, cutting off the "tentacles." Slice the kohlrabi into rounds 1 inch thick. In a bamboo or metal steamer, steam the rounds for 3 minutes. Put them in a bowl and sprinkle with salt and black pepper to taste. Set aside to cool. When cool, pour the Anchovy Vinaigrette over the kohlrabi and toss.

In a large saucepan, place the water, wine, onion and bay leaf. Bring to a boil and simmer for 5 minutes. Add the bluefish fillets, bring the liquid back to a boil, reduce the heat and simmer for 6 minutes or just until the fish flakes easily with a fork; do not overcook the fish. With 2 spatulas, remove the fillets to a large platter to cool.

Fit a pastry bag with a small tube and fill the bag with the Mayonnaise. Pipe small mayonnaise roses around the fish fillets. Top with the thin lime slices and sprinkle with chopped dill. Surround the fish with circles of the marinated kohlrabi and serve.

Meat

Beef

Meat

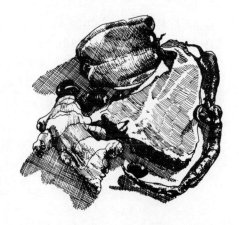

Beef

🍖 Lucy's Pot Roast 🍖

Serves 8

*L*ucy is my housekeeper; she has been with me for 25 years. She is famous among my friends for making the best pot roast in town. Every year, Lucy's pot roast has some new dimension. Lucy keeps abreast of the latest trends, and has served us pot roast with green peppercorns, with cranberries and now with star fruit. Every one of her inventions is a success. The following recipe is made with both green peppercorns and star fruit. If you are lucky enough to have some pot roast left over, it is superb served cold with Horseradish Sauce (see page 238).

3 carrots, scraped and diced
2 large onions, sliced
1 celery stalk, cut into small pieces
4 garlic cloves, chopped
1 teaspoon kosher salt
1 teaspoon freshly ground black pepper
½ teaspoon dried thyme
½ teaspoon ground cumin
1 cup dry white wine
5 tablespoons vegetable oil
2 tablespoons lemon juice

6 pounds lean beef brisket
3 tablespoons olive oil
1 onion, stuck with 1 clove
2 garlic cloves, sliced
3 garlic cloves, slivered
2 cups Beef Stock (see page 46)
2 tablespoons drained green peppercorns
3 star fruit or carambolas, sliced
chopped parsley, for garnish

In a large deep bowl, combine the carrots, sliced onions, celery, chopped garlic, salt, black pepper, thyme, cumin, wine, vegetable oil and lemon juice. Mix well. Add the meat to marinate. Refrigerate overnight, turning the meat once or twice.

In a large heavy saucepan, heat the olive oil over high heat. Add the whole onion stuck with 1 clove and the sliced garlic. Reduce the heat and gently sauté until lightly golden brown. Remove from the heat.

Remove the meat from the marinade. With a sharp knife, make holes in it and insert the garlic slivers.

Heat the oil in the saucepan again. Add the meat and brown it on all sides over high heat.

Add the marinade and the beef stock. Bring to a boil and lower the heat. Add the green peppercorns, cover and simmer for 2 hours or until the meat is easily pierced with a fork.

Remove the meat from the saucepan and let cool.

Slice the meat and return it to the saucepan. Add the sliced star fruit and simmer for 5 minutes.

With a spatula, remove the meat to a large platter. Garnish with the star fruit slices. Pour some sauce over the meat, garnish with parsley, and pass the remaining sauce in a sauceboat.

❦ New York Potée ❦

Serves 8

Potée is a dish of boiled meats with lots of vegetables, served with two or three different sauces. To serve this dish on the grandest scale, you need at least eight guests. The dish is a meal in itself; serve the soup, the meats and the vegetables as one course with fresh rye bread or pumpernickel.

3 pounds beef soup bones
4 beef marrow bones
5 quarts water
1 pound chicken gizzards,
    wings and/or necks
3 pounds beef brisket
6 garlic cloves, peeled
8 short ribs of beef, about
    2 pounds
1 large onion, stuck with
    2 cloves
2 bay leaves
2 sprigs fresh thyme or
    ½ teaspoon dried thyme
salt
1 tablespoon black
    peppercorns
1 kosher Romanian garlic
    sausage, sliced

1 chicken, about 2½ pounds
8 medium potatoes, peeled
    and quartered
8 small turnips, peeled
8 small parsnips
1 acorn squash, about
    1½ pounds, peeled,
    seeded and cubed
1 large head cabbage
3 bunches scallions, trimmed
    and tied together with
    string, or 8 leeks,
    washed, trimmed and
    tied together with string
8 small carrots, scraped and
    trimmed
8 small zucchinis, trimmed
1 pound stuffed derma,
    sliced

Condiments:
1 cup Aïoli (see page 237)
1 cup Sweet Red Pepper
    Sauce (see page 235)

grated horseradish
kosher salt
Dijon mustard

Wash the beef bones and the marrow bones. Place them in a very large pot and add the water. Bring to a boil, uncovered. Lower the heat and skim the surface. Add the chicken gizzards, bring to a boil again, lower the heat and skim the surface. Cook for 25 minutes. With a slotted spoon, remove the marrow bones and place them on a large heatproof platter. Keep warm. Remove and discard the beef soup bones and chicken gizzards.

Cut 3 slits in the beef brisket and insert a garlic clove into each. Rub the short ribs with 2 garlic cloves. Add the brisket and ribs to the stock. Bring to a boil, reduce the heat and skim the surface. Add the onion, remaining garlic, bay leaves, thyme, salt to taste and the peppercorns. Bring to a boil again and simmer for 1 ½ hours, partially covered, skimming the top from time to time.

Add the garlic sausage and the chicken. Bring to a boil, reduce the heat, skim the surface and simmer for 25 minutes.

Add the potatoes and turnips; cook for 10 minutes.

Add the parsnips and acorn squash and cook for 10 minutes more.

Meanwhile, place the cabbage in another saucepan. With a ladle, add 4 cups of the stock; bring to a boil, reduce the heat and simmer for 15 minutes. Turn off the heat and let the cabbage stand in the broth.

Add the scallions or leeks, carrots and zucchini to the soup pot. Bring to a boil, lower the heat and simmer for 5 minutes.

Add the stuffed derma slices and cook until just heated through, about 2 to 3 minutes.

At this point, the meats and vegetables can be removed to the platter with the marrow bones; pour 2 cups of the soup over the meats and vegetables, cover with aluminum foil and place in a 200°F oven to keep warm. The soup can be kept warm over very low heat on top of the stove.

To serve, remove all the meats to a carving board. Carve the brisket and arrange the slices on one side of a large platter. Cut the chicken into 8 serving pieces and arrange them alongside the brisket. On the other side of the platter, place the short ribs and sliced garlic sausage; in the center, arrange the marrow bones. Pour some soup over all the meat and garnish with the parsley. On a separate round platter, arrange the vegetables, placing the cabbage head in the center. Strain the remaining soup through a fine sieve placed over a large saucepan. Heat the soup just before serving. Serve a bowl of hot soup to each guest, along with the meats and vegetables, and condiments in small bowls so that each guest can help himself.

❦ Parmentier ❦

Serves 6

*P*armentier! The word evokes my favorite meal as a
child. Sunday evening was the cook's night out. She
always prepared a parmentier, layers of meat covered
with a potato purée, on Sunday morning before she left. The
only thing we had to do was bake it in the oven. Monsieur
Parmentier was a famous eighteenth-century chemist who
was asked by the French government to develop recipes for
the potato, which had been introduced in France without any
success. For this dish, use leftover meat, preferably boiled
beef or pot roast.

1 pound leftover boiled beef
 or Pot Roast (see
 page 124)
2 tablespoons olive oil
½ pound white mushrooms,
 coarsely chopped
½ pound fresh shelled peas
½ cup leftover sauce from
 the meat, or ½ cup Beef
 Stock (see page 46)

salt
freshly ground black pepper
2 pounds potatoes, peeled
 and quartered
2 eggs, beaten
½ cake silken bean curd
⅛ teaspoon nutmeg
1 egg yolk, beaten

Preheat the oven to 425°F.
    Cut the leftover meat into 1-inch cubes and coarsely chop
them.
    In a large skillet, heat the oil over medium-high heat. Add
the mushrooms and sauté until they are light brown; add the
meat, peas and sauce or beef stock. Sprinkle with salt and
black pepper to taste, reduce the heat and simmer,
uncovered, for 5 minutes. Remove from the heat and set
aside.
    Place the potatoes in a saucepan and add just enough

water to cover them. Add ½ teaspoon salt. Bring to a boil, reduce the heat to medium and cook for 15 minutes or until the potatoes are easily pierced with a fork. Drain the potatoes and place them in a food processor. Add the eggs, bean curd, nutmeg and salt and black pepper to taste. Process until the ingredients are puréed.

Fill a 2-quart baking dish with the meat-and-mushroom mixture, including the sauce. Cover with the potato purée. At this point the dish can be refrigerated until needed, even overnight. When ready to bake, brush the top of the purée with the egg yolk. Bake for 20 minutes, or until the top of the purée is golden brown.

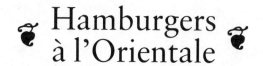

Hamburgers à l'Orientale

Serves 4

2 pounds lean chopped beef	salt
6 garlic cloves, chopped	freshly ground black pepper
4 small onions, chopped	½ cup all-purpose flour
2 egg whites, beaten	4 tablespoons vegetable oil
¼ teaspoon nutmeg	1 cup Tahini Sauce (see
¼ teaspoon ground cumin	page 231)

In a mixing bowl, combine the beef, garlic, onions, egg whites, nutmeg, cumin and salt and black pepper to taste. Mix well and form into 4 hamburgers. Dredge the hamburgers lightly in the flour.

In a large skillet, heat the oil over high heat. Add the hamburgers and cook for 3 minutes or until the bottoms are browned. Turn them over, lower the heat and cook 5 minutes more for rare meat and longer for more well-done meat. Serve with the Tahini Sauce on the side.

ᷡ Roast Beef with ᷡ Tarragon Sauce

Serves 6

In this recipe the beef is marinated overnight with papaya to tenderize it naturally.

1 3¼-pound center-cut lean chuck roast
1 papaya, peeled and thinly sliced
3 tablespoons olive oil
2 tablespoons chopped fresh tarragon or 2 teaspoons dried tarragon

3 garlic cloves, chopped
salt
freshly ground black pepper
1 cup Beef Stock (see page 46)
2 tablespoons soy sauce or low-sodium soy sauce
1 cup water

Place the roast in a large roasting pan. Cover it with the papaya slices, cover with aluminum foil and refrigerate overnight.

Preheat the oven to 400°F.

In a small bowl, mix together the olive oil, tarragon, garlic and salt and black pepper to taste.

Remove and discard the papaya slices from the roast. Pour the tarragon mixture over the roast. Pour the Beef Stock and the soy sauce into the roasting pan. Roast the beef for 1 hour.

Remove the roast to a carving board and let it stand 10 minutes before carving. Slice it very thinly and arrange the slices on a serving platter.

Add the water to the juices in the roasting pan. Bring the gravy to a boil on top of the stove. Pour it over the beef slices.

Thomas's Stuffed Meat Loaf

Serves 6

M y son hated meat loaf. I love it. One day I made a meat loaf with capers, hard-boiled eggs and lots of garlic, and begged him to try it. The meat loaf was such a success that it disappeared in one meal. My son, now in college, is the manager of the college cafeteria. One day he called for my meat loaf recipe. The students loved it so much that it got him a raise! This meat loaf is even better cold, served with strong Dijon mustard and French cornichons or sliced sour pickles.

1 pound chopped beef	3 tablespoons chopped
1 pound chopped veal	parsley
1 pound chopped chicken	3 tablespoons drained
2 eggs	capers
2 tablespoons duck or	5 hard-boiled eggs, peeled
chicken fat	16 pimento-stuffed green
2 slices white bread	olives
salt	3 garlic cloves, slivered
freshly ground black pepper	3 cups Chicken Stock (see
4 shallots, chopped	page 49)
	parsley sprigs, for garnish

Preheat the oven to 350°F.

In a large mixing bowl, combine the chopped meats, eggs and duck fat. Mix well.

Dip the bread in cold water and squeeze out the liquid. Add the bread to the meat and mix well again. Add the shallots, parsley, capers and salt and black pepper to taste. Mix well and taste the mixture to see if it is spicy enough. (If you don't like to taste raw meat, make a little ball and poach it in boiling water for 1 minute.)

Form the mixture into a loaf about 9 inches long and 5 inches wide. Place the loaf in a large baking pan. With your fingers, open the loaf along the center. Place the hard-boiled eggs in the center in a row and surround the eggs with the olives. Reshape the meat mixture to enclose the eggs and olives completely. Push the garlic slivers into the surface of the loaf.

Pour the Chicken Stock into the baking pan. Bake, basting from time to time, for 1½ hours.

Remove the loaf to a serving platter and slice. Garnish with parsley sprigs.

Scrape the edges of the baking dish and add more water to the liquid if necessary to make about 2 cups of sauce. Correct the seasoning. Pour the sauce into a sauceboat and serve with the meat.

Veal

❧ Roast Veal ❧

Serves 6

*T*his roast veal is excellent cold. To serve it cold, remove the sliced meat from the liquid, place it on a platter, cover with aluminum foil and refrigerate. Pour the cooking liquid and vegetables through a strainer into a bowl and refrigerate. Reheat the sauce and serve it with the veal.

1 5-pound veal roast
3 garlic cloves, thinly sliced
4 tablespoons olive oil
2 tablespoons light soy
   sauce or low-sodium soy
   sauce
1 tablespoon lemon juice
salt
freshly ground black pepper
2 to 3 cups Chicken Stock
   (see page 49)

1 cup dry white wine
2 onions, sliced
1 bay leaf
2 sprigs fresh rosemary
1 head Boston lettuce
1½ pounds small new
   potatoes
3 carrots, scraped and cut
   into 1-inch pieces
2 10-ounce packages frozen
   tiny peas

With the tip of a sharp knife, make slits in the veal roast and insert slivers of garlic.

In a large mixing bowl, mix together 2 tablespoons of the olive oil, the soy sauce, lemon juice and salt and black pepper to taste. Add the veal roast and marinate for 2 hours.

In a Dutch oven, heat the remaining olive oil over medium heat. Add the onions and sauté until transparent.

Remove the veal from the marinade and add it to the Dutch oven; reserve the marinade. Raise the heat and brown the roast on all sides. Add the marinade, 2 cups of the Chicken Stock, the white wine, onion, rosemary and bay leaf. Cover the meat with lettuce leaves. Bring to a boil, reduce the heat, cover and simmer for 1 hour.

Add the potatoes and carrots. Add more chicken stock if needed (the veal roast should be one-third covered with liquid). Simmer, covered, for another 2 hours or until the meat is easily pierced with a fork. Turn off the heat and let the meat cool in its juices.

Remove the roast from the Dutch oven and slice. Add the lettuce leaves to the other vegetables or discard. Place the veal slices back in the Dutch oven on top of the vegetables; add the frozen peas and gently reheat until the peas are warmed through. Serve in the Dutch oven.

❦ Veal in Jelly ❦

Serves 6

2 tablespoons vegetable oil
2 pounds boneless veal,
 cubed
salt
freshly ground black pepper
4 cups water
1 tablespoon chopped fresh
 thyme or 1½ teaspoons
 dried thyme

1 bay leaf
4 hard-boiled eggs, halved
 lengthwise and sliced
2 cups cooked green peas
watercress sprigs, for
 garnish
Horseradish Sauce (see
 page 238)

In a large saucepan, heat the oil over medium heat. Add the meat and brown on all sides. Sprinkle with salt and black pepper to taste. Add the water, thyme and bay leaf. Lower the heat and simmer, covered, for 2 hours or until the meat is tender enough to be cut with a fork.

Oil a 2-quart round mold. Arrange the egg slices in a circle in the bottom of mold.

Remove the bay leaf from the veal. Place a layer of veal over the eggs; top with a layer of peas, another layer of veal and another layer of peas. Pour the cooking liquid over the meat and refrigerate several hours until the liquid has set.

Just before serving, pass the blade of a knife all around the edges of the mold. Place a serving platter upside down over the top of the mold, invert them together, and unmold onto the platter. Garnish with watercress sprigs and serve with Horseradish Sauce.

Veal Roast with Marinated Artichokes

Serves 6 to 8

This veal can be served hot or cold. When serving it hot, you must let the meat rest for about 15 minutes before carving, so that it will not fall apart. Serve with steamed asparagus.

1 4-pound center-cut veal shoulder, boned and tied
4 garlic cloves, cut into slivers
2 tablespoons margarine
1 pound pearl onions, peeled
1 cup Chicken Stock (see page 49) or water

1 tablespoon dark soy sauce or low-sodium soy sauce
salt
freshly ground black pepper
2 sprigs fresh thyme or ½ teaspoon dried thyme
2 6-ounce jars marinated artichoke hearts

With the point of a small, sharp knife, make slits in the veal. Insert the garlic slivers.

In a saucepan large enough to hold the veal roast easily, melt the margarine over high heat. Add the veal and brown it on all sides. Lower the heat to medium, add the pearl onions and cook for 4 minutes. Add the Chicken Stock and soy sauce and salt and black pepper to taste. Place the thyme sprigs on top of the meat. Cover, lower the heat and simmer for 1 hour.

Add the artichokes with their marinade and simmer for 45 minutes, or until the meat is easily pierced with a fork.

If the veal is to be eaten hot, remove it to a carving board and let it stand for 15 minutes. Slice it and arrange the slices on a platter. Pour the sauce over the meat.

If the veal is to be eaten cold, leave it in the saucepan and refrigerate. To serve, slice the meat and arrange it on a platter. Warm the sauce and pour it over the slices.

❦ Stuffed Breast of Veal ❦

Serves 6

My stepfather was from Normandy. He was a man of few words, except when talking about the regional dishes of his homeland. When the conversation veered to breast of veal, his favorite dish, his language became genuinely poetic. This recipe is based on his. Serve it with steamed Brussels sprouts and mashed potatoes. Serve the leftovers cold with strong Dijon mustard and steamed string beans. Have your butcher cut a pocket in the breast of veal for stuffing.

1 6-pound veal breast, with
    pocket cut for stuffing
salt
freshly ground black pepper
2 garlic cloves, halved

2 tablespoons dark soy
    sauce or low-sodium soy
    sauce
1 bunch watercress for
    garnish

Stuffing:
3 pounds beef marrow
    bones
4 tablespoons vegetable oil
1 pound fresh chicken livers,
    trimmed
salt
freshly ground black pepper
2 tablespoons brandy
2 slices white bread
½ cup white wine
1 pound chopped veal
½ pound mushrooms,
    coarsely chopped

½ pound fresh sorrel,
    trimmed and coarsely
    chopped
2 garlic cloves, chopped
1 tablespoon chopped fresh
    parsley
1 teaspoon dried thyme
1 teaspoon fresh tarragon
    leaves or ½ teaspoon
    dried tarragon
2 egg yolks

Cooking Liquid:

2 carrots, peeled and thinly
   sliced
2 onions, quartered

2 veal bones, cracked
3 cups Chicken Stock (see
   page 49)

Wipe the veal breast with paper towels. Rub the pocket and the outsides of the meat with the garlic clove halves; discard the garlic. Sprinkle the meat all over with salt and black pepper and brush the top with the soy sauce. Set the meat aside.

To prepare the stuffing, wash the marrow bones. Place them in a large saucepan and add enough cold water to cover. Bring the water to a boil, reduce the heat to medium and cook, uncovered, for 8 minutes. Gently remove the bones with tongs and place them in large bowl to cool. When cool enough to handle, tap the bones gently; the marrow will fall out. Use a sharp, narrow knife to remove any marrow that remains in the bones. Place the marrow in a bowl, cover and refrigerate for 1 hour.

In a medium skillet, heat 1 tablespoon of the vegetable oil over medium-high heat. Add the livers, sprinkle them with salt and black pepper to taste, reduce the heat to medium and sauté, stirring often, until they are just firm and lightly browned. Pour the brandy over the livers and carefully ignite it with a match. Gently stir the livers with a wooden spoon until the flames die away. Remove the skillet from the heat. When the livers are cool enough to handle, cut them into ½-inch pieces.

In a small bowl, soak the bread slices in the wine. Squeeze the bread to remove the excess wine; reserve the wine.

Put the marrow, chicken livers and bread in a large mixing bowl. Add chopped veal, mushrooms, sorrel, garlic, parsley, thyme, tarragon and egg yolks. Season to taste with salt and black pepper and mix well.

Preheat the oven to 425°F.

Fill the pocket of the veal breast with the stuffing, packing it in tightly. Sew or skewer the pocket closed.

Place the stuffed veal breast in a large roasting pan. Brush it with the remaining oil. Surround the veal with the carrots, onions and cracked veal bones. Pour the Chicken Stock and reserved bread-soaking wine into the pan.

Roast the veal for 15 minutes, or until the top of the meat is browned. Baste it well with the pan liquids and cover loosely with aluminum foil. Reduce the oven temperature to 375°F and roast for 2½ hours, basting occasionally. (Add some water to the roasting pan if the liquid evaporates too quickly.)

To serve, carve the veal into slices, between the ribs, and arrange on a large serving platter. Garnish with the watercress. Serve the pan juices on the side in a sauceboat.

Veal with Passion Fruit

Serves 6

Passion fruit is a round purple-skinned fruit, about the size of a kiwi fruit, full of small seeds surrounded by a transparent juicy pulp. The sweet, slightly tart fruit is excellent in a sauce for poultry or meat. Pleurotes are large light gray mushrooms. If they are not available, use very large cultivated mushrooms instead.

2 passion fruit
12 thin veal scallops
¼ cup all-purpose flour
3 tablespoons vegetable oil
2 shallots, chopped
salt
freshly ground black pepper

2 cups Chicken Stock (see page 49)
2 sprigs fresh thyme or 1 teaspoon dried thyme
1 pound pleurotes
watercress sprigs, for garnish

138

Cut the passion fruit in half lengthwise and scoop out the seeds and pulp. Place them in a strainer over a bowl and press with the back of a soup spoon to extract the juice. Discard the seeds; reserve the juice.

Dredge the veal scallops in the flour. Shake off any excess.

In a large skillet, heat the oil over medium-high heat. Add the shallots and sauté for 3 minutes or until they are transparent but not browned. Add the veal scallops and brown them on both sides. Sprinkle with salt and black pepper to taste. Add the Chicken Stock and the thyme. Bring to a boil, then lower the heat and simmer for 3 minutes.

Remove the veal to a platter.

Strain the contents of the skillet through a fine sieve into a food processor and purée. Pour the sauce back into the skillet and add the pleurotes. Cook for 5 minutes and add the passion fruit juice. Cook gently until the sauce is heated through; do not let it boil. Pour the sauce over the veal, garnish with watercress sprigs and serve.

❦ Stuffed Lettuce Leaves ❦

Serves 6

I have always liked stuffed vegetables. In the summer, my mother would stuff zucchini with leftover chicken or beef. She cooked them in a very lemony sauce and served them cold. My mother-in-law's speciality was stuffed cabbage leaves cooked in a sweet-and-sour sauce, a recipe she had learned from a Hungarian friend. My own speciality is to stuff lettuce leaves, an excellent alternative to cabbage. I like to serve it with couscous or the rice-shaped pasta known as orzo.

139

2 slices white bread
½ cup Chicken Stock (see
   page 000)
2 pounds chopped veal
4 eggs
1 bunch parsley, stemmed
¼ teaspoon cumin
⅛ teaspoon nutmeg
salt
freshly ground black pepper
½ cup all-purpose flour

3 tablespoons vegetable oil
2 heads Boston lettuce
3 tablespoons olive oil
2 onions, thinly sliced
2 garlic cloves, sliced
1 1-pound can peeled Italian
   tomatoes
6 medium basil leaves or
   ½ teaspoon dried basil
½ teaspoon dried oregano

In a bowl, soak the bread in the Chicken Stock for 10 minutes. Squeeze the bread to remove excess liquid. Discard the stock.

Place the bread, veal, eggs, parsley leaves, cumin and nutmeg in a food processor. Process until the ingredients are finely chopped. Remove to a large mixing bowl and add salt and black pepper to taste. Mix well.

From the veal mixture into balls about 2 inches in diameter.

Spread the flour on a plate. Dredge the meatballs in flour and shake off any excess.

In a large skillet, heat the vegetable oil over medium-high heat. Add the meatballs and brown them on all sides. Lower the heat and sauté gently, uncovered, for 8 minutes. Turn off the heat and set aside.

Separate the lettuce leaves and wash them well. Drain well. Place the leaves in a large bowl, saving the small leaves of the lettuce hearts for a salad. Pour into the bowl enough boiling water to cover the leaves. Immediately drain well and pat the leaves dry with paper towels.

Place a meat ball in the center of each lettuce leaf. Roll up the leaves to enclose the meat, just as if you were making stuffed cabbage (see the illustration on page 000).

In another skillet, heat the olive oil over medium-high heat. Add the onions and the garlic, lower the heat and sauté until the onions are transparent but not browned. Add the tomatoes with their juice, the basil, oregano and salt and black pepper to taste. Bring to a boil, lower the heat and simmer, uncovered, for 1 hour, stirring from time to time and adding more water if necessary. The sauce should have the consistency of a thin purée.

Preheat the oven to 350°F.

Pour the tomato sauce into a large baking dish. Place the stuffed lettuce leaves on top and bake for 30 minutes. Serve from the baking pan.

Sweetbreads with Three-Color Peppers

Serves 6

G reen peppers were, for a long time, the only bell peppers available in the United States. Then the Dutch, with their love of color and flowers, developed new peppers in several brilliant colors, reminiscent of their tulips. Today nearly every market carries yellow, purple and sometimes even white sweet peppers along with the traditional green and red ones. In this recipe, I use three colors (my father always told me three was a good number): red, yellow and purple. Placed among the peppers are sautéed slices of sweetbread.

2 veal sweetbreads, about 1½ pounds
2 yellow sweet peppers
2 red sweet peppers
2 purple sweet peppers
½ cup flour
salt
freshly ground black pepper

4 to 6 tablespoons vegetable oil
3 shallots, chopped
2 teaspoons Dijon mustard
½ cup Chicken Stock (see page 49)
1 tablespoon dried tarragon

141

Sweetbreads are covered with a very thin membrane. Using a sharp knife, remove most of the membrane and any gristle attached to the sweetbreads. Wash them and pat dry with paper towels. Place the sweetbreads on a plate, then put another plate on top. Weight the plate down with a can or two and let stand for 30 minutes to press out excess liquid from the sweetbreads.

Cut all the peppers into rings 1¼ inch wide. Remove the seeds. Set aside.

Drain the sweetbreads, pat them dry and cut them into 1-inch slices. Place the flour on a plate, add salt and black pepper to taste and mix with your fingers. Dredge the sweetbread slices in the flour; shake them to remove any excess flour.

In a medium skillet heat 4 tablespoons of the oil over high heat. Add the shallots, lower the heat to medium and sauté until they are transparent but not browned. Add the sweetbreads and sauté until golden brown; turn and cook until the other side is golden brown. Remove the sweetbreads and shallots to a plate and keep warm in a low oven while cooking the peppers.

Add more oil to the skillet, if necessary. When the oil is hot, add the peppers and sauté for 3 minutes on each side, until hot but still crisp (the crunchy texture of the peppers contrasts nicely with the softness of the sweetbreads).

With a fork, remove the pepper rings one by one and arrange them on a round platter, mixing the colors. Place the sweetbreads on top of the peppers. Keep warm while preparing the sauce.

Add the Chicken Stock to the skillet. Bring to a boil and add the mustard and tarragon. Mix well, reduce the heat and simmer for 2 minutes. Pour the sauce over the sweetbreads and serve immediately.

Blanquette de Veau (Veal Stew with Lemon)

Serves 6

This dish can be kept warm in a very low oven overnight, or made several days in advance and refrigerated. Blanquette de veau freezes very well. Serve with steamed potatoes and a salad.

2 tablespoons goose or chicken fat

1 3½-pound boneless veal breast, cut into 1-inch cubes

2 tablespoons all-purpose flour

about 2 quarts Chicken Stock (see page 49)

2 carrots, cut into 1-inch pieces

2 onions, each stuck with 1 clove

5 black peppercorns

1 ounce dried Polish mushrooms, soaked for 10 minutes in ¼ cup cold water

2 sprigs fresh rosemary or ½ teaspoon dried rosemary

1 bay leaf

salt

freshly ground black pepper

1 pound small white mushrooms, trimmed

1 egg

about 3 tablespoons lemon juice

In a very large saucepan, melt the goose fat over medium heat. Add the veal pieces and lightly brown on all sides. Sprinkle with the flour and mix well.

Slowly add enough Chicken Stock to cover the veal completely. Bring to a boil, reduce the heat to medium, and add the carrots, onions, peppercorns, Polish mushrooms

143

with their liquid, rosemary, bay leaf and salt and black pepper to taste. Simmer, covered, for 2 hours.

Add the white mushrooms 10 minutes before serving.

Just before serving, beat together the egg and lemon juice in a mixing bowl. Slowly beat in 1 cup of the veal cooking liquid. Pour the egg mixture back into the veal stew. Add more lemon juice if desired; the stew should be very lemony.

Lamb

❦ Lamb Spareribs ❦

Serves 6

A couple of years ago, I met a fish wholesaler who had decided to open a fish restaurant near the Fulton Fish Market. His wife wanted him to serve chicken and spareribs, too. But since she kept kosher, no pork! He came up with this wonderful recipe for lamb spareribs, and it made his restaurant very successful. Serve with corn on the cob or baked beans.

1 lamb breast, with excess
  fat trimmed off
6 tablespoons dark soy
  sauce or low-sodium soy
  sauce
6 tablespoons sugar
1 tablespoon sesame oil

3 tablespoons olive oil
6 tablespoons water
2 tablespoons grated ginger
4 garlic cloves, crushed
½ teaspoon cracked black
  peppercorns
1 tablespoon kosher salt

Cut the lamb breast along the bones to separate it into individual ribs.

In a bowl, mix all the remaining ingredients together.

Place the ribs in a baking pan and cover them with the sauce. Let the ribs marinate at room temperature for at least 2 hours.

Preheat the oven to 300°F.

Bake the spareribs for 1 hour, basting frequently.

❦ Roast Shoulder ❦
of Lamb

Serves 6

*A*sk the butcher to prepare the shoulder of lamb for you by cutting a pocket between the skin and the meat, just as if preparing a veal breast for stuffing. Or you can do it yourself with a sharp knife, starting at one end and sliding the knife between the skin and the meat. Once you have started to cut the meat away, the skin will easily separate from the meat.

1 boneless lamb shoulder, with pocket
2 garlic cloves, chopped
salt
freshly ground black pepper
½ pound short-grain rice
¼ pound chopped beef
1 ½ tablespoons lemon juice

1 teaspoon chopped parsley
¼ teaspoon ground cumin
2 tablespoons olive oil
2 cups Beef Stock (see page 46), Chicken Stock (see page 49) or water
parsley sprigs, for garnish

145

Preheat the oven to 375°F.

Rub the lamb with the garlic inside and out. Sprinkle with salt and black pepper to taste.

In a large bowl, mix the rice with the chopped beef. Add salt and black pepper to taste and the lemon juice, chopped parsley and cumin. Mix well with your hands. Lightly stuff the lamb pocket with the mixture. Do not pack it too tightly, as the rice will expand as it cooks. Sew the pocket closed with a heavy needle and heavy white cotton thread.

Place the stuffed shoulder in a roasting pan. Brush with olive oil and add the Beef Stock to the pan.

Lower the oven temperature to 350°F. Bake for 3 hours, basting the meat frequently. Add more stock if necessary; there should be ½ cup of liquid in the roasting pan at all times.

Remove from the oven and let the roast stand for 10 minutes before carving.

Place the meat on a serving platter. Garnish with parsley sprigs.

Add ½ cup of water to the roasting pan and scrape the sides. Bring to a boil on the stove top. Add salt and black pepper to taste, reduce the heat and simmer for 3 minutes. Pour the gravy into a sauceboat.

৶ Lamb Stew ৶ with Apples

Serves 4

2 tablespoons vegetable oil
2 pounds boneless lamb
   shoulder, cubed
1 tablespoon mild curry
   powder
salt
freshly ground black pepper

about 1 cup Chicken Stock
   (see page 49) or water
4 green apples, peeled, cored
   and quartered
2 onions, chopped
1 cake silken bean curd

In a large saucepan, heat the oil over high heat. Add the lamb cubes and sauté until browned. Sprinkle with the curry powder and salt and black pepper to taste. Mix well and add the Chicken Stock. Bring to a boil, lower the heat, cover and cook for 15 minutes.

Add the apples and onions. Bring to a boil again, lower the heat and simmer for 40 minutes. Add more Chicken Stock if necessary; there should be about ½ cup of liquid in the saucepan.

With a slotted spoon, remove the meat and apples and put them on a serving platter.

Place the sauce with the onions in a food processor. Add the bean curd and process until the ingredients are puréed. Pour the sauce back into the saucepan. Add more salt and black pepper if necessary. Gently heat the sauce; do not let it boil. Pour the sauce over the meat and apples and serve with steamed rice or noodles.

🫖 Lamb Stew with Celery 🫖 Root and Cherries

Serves 6

2 tablespoons olive oil	1 carrot, sliced
2 onions, each stuck with	1 bouquet garni
1 clove	salt
2 garlic cloves	freshly ground black pepper
2 pounds boneless lamb, cut	2 celery roots, peeled and
into 1-inch pieces	cut into large dice
1 tablespoon all-purpose	1 pound pearl onions,
flour	peeled
4 cups Chicken Stock (see	18 brandied cherries
page 49)	parsley sprigs, for garnish

In a large saucepan, heat the oil over medium-high heat. Add the onions and garlic cloves. Sauté for 5 minutes, or until the onions are lightly browned. Add the lamb pieces and brown them on all sides. Sprinkle the flour over the lamb and mix well. Add the Chicken Stock, carrot and bouquet garni. Sprinkle with salt and black pepper to taste. Bring the stew to a boil, reduce the heat and simmer, covered, for 35 minutes. Add the celery root and cook, covered, for another 20 minutes.

    With a slotted spoon, remove the lamb and the vegetables to a platter. Strain the sauce into a saucepan. Cook the sauce over high heat for 5 minutes; add the pearl onions and cook for 10 minutes longer. Drain the cherries (reserve the liquid for an after-dinner drink) and add them to the sauce. Cook 2 minutes longer. Pour the sauce over the lamb, garnish with parsley sprigs and serve.

Yakitori of Lamb and Chicken

Serves 4

Yakitori is the Japanese version of kebabs—broiled meats and vegetables on skewers, brushed with a Teriyaki Sauce made with sake and dark soy sauce (see page 232). In this recipe, I combine my grandmother's old Turkish recipe for shaslik with a yakitori I learned in Japan.

1 bay leaf
1 teaspoon crushed dried
   thyme
2 tablespoons olive oil
2 tablespoons lime juice
zest of 1 lime, grated
1/8 teaspoon cayenne pepper
salt
freshly ground black pepper
1 pound boneless lamb
   shoulder, cubed

1 large chicken breast,
   boned and cubed
1 sweet red pepper, cut into
   1-inch pieces
1 green pepper, cut into
   1-inch pieces
16 white mushroom caps
1 cup Teriyaki Sauce (see
   page 232)

Crush the bay leaf and mix it with the thyme in a bowl; add the olive oil, lime juice, lime zest, cayenne pepper and salt and black pepper to taste. Mix the marinade well.

   In another large bowl, place the lamb and chicken cubes. Pour the marinade over them, mix well and let stand at cool room temperature for 12 hours.

   Preheat the broiler.

   On each of 16 bamboo or metal skewers, put 1 piece each of chicken, sweet red pepper, lamb, green pepper, and then a mushroom cap. Brush with the Teriyaki Sauce and broil on one side for 6 minutes; turn over, baste with more Teriyaki Sauce and broil for 6 more minutes.

❧ Boned Shoulder ❧ of Lamb

Serves 6

W *hen you want to make this dish, it's a good idea prepare the stuffing first and take it with you to the butcher's. When he bones the shoulder of lamb for you, ask him nicely to place the stuffing in the center before rolling the meat. Also ask for the bones; they make a marvelous gravy for the meat. (If you haven't made friends with your butcher, you can easily stuff the roast yourself. All you need is good kitchen string and a little patience.)*

Cooking Liquid:
2 tablespoons olive oil
lamb shoulder bones, cut into small pieces
1 carrot, sliced
1 boned lamb shoulder
salt
black pepper

2 garlic cloves, slivered
10 shiso leaves or 10 mint leaves
1 celery stalk, sliced
salt
freshly ground black pepper
4 cups water

Stuffing:
2 tablespoons olive oil
1 pound chicken livers, trimmed and cut into small pieces
1 cup shelled unsalted pistachio nuts
2 onions, chopped
2 fennel bulbs, trimmed and julienned

1 egg
½ cup coarse unflavored breadcrumbs
2 tablespoons chopped parsley
salt
black pepper
1 lime zest, julienned

150

In a large skillet, heat the oil over medium heat. Add the lamb shoulder bones and brown on all sides. Add the carrot and celery and salt and black pepper to taste. Cook over medium heat for 5 minutes. Add the water, bring to a boil, reduce the heat and simmer for 30 minutes. Correct the seasoning. Pour the liquid through a strainer into a saucepan and set aside while preparing the meat.

Spread the lamb shoulder on the work surface. Sprinkle the inside with salt and black pepper to taste. With a sharp knife, make small holes in the meat and insert the garlic slivers. Arrange the shiso or mint leaves side by side, covering most of the area where the stuffing will be placed. Set aside while preparing the stuffing.

Preheat the oven to 425°F.

In the same skillet used to prepare the cooking liquid, heat the oil over medium-high heat. Add the chicken livers and sauté for 5 minutes. Add the pistachio nuts, onions and fennel and sauté for 5 minutes. Remove the mixture to a large mixing bowl. Add the egg, breadcrumbs, parsley, salt and black pepper to taste and the lime zest. Mix well and spread the mixture on top of the leaves. Roll the meat, enclosing the stuffing, as you would a jelly roll. Tie the meat with kitchen string every 3 inches (see illustration).

Place the stuffed lamb shoulder in a large baking dish. Pour the reserved broth over the meat and bake for 1 hour, basting from time to time. Remove from the oven and let stand for 15 minutes before slicing.

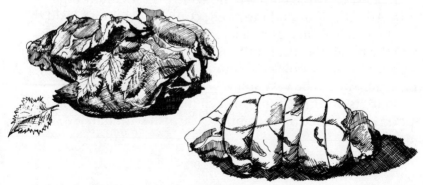

❧ Broiled Lamb Chops ❧ with Hot Pimentos

Serves 4

*C*ount on two double lamb chops per person. Serve this with hot French bread.

8 double lamb chops
2 tablespoons margarine
1 tablespoon all-purpose
    flour
1 cup Chicken Stock (see
    page 49)
1 tablespoon wine vinegar
½ tablespoon lemon juice
2 hot red pimentos, thickly
    sliced

½ pound pearl onions,
    peeled, or ½ pound
    frozen pearl onions
1 tablespoon drained capers
salt
freshly ground black pepper
parsley sprigs, for garnish

Preheat the broiler until it is very hot.

Broil the lamb chops for 3 minutes; lower the heat and broil for 6 to 10 minutes, depending on the degree of doneness desired.

In a saucepan, melt the margarine over medium-high heat. Add the flour and mix well; cook for 1 minute. Add the Chicken Stock, vinegar and lemon juice, stirring constantly. Add the pimentos, pearl onions, capers and salt and black pepper to taste. Cook for 4 minutes. Correct the seasoning; the sauce should be very spicy.

Place two lamb chops on each individual serving plate. Spoon some sauce on each plate. Garnish with parsley sprigs and serve.

Marinated Broiled Lamb Chops

Serves 6

*T*his is a very simple dish that is also very elegant. Serve with Braised Salsify (see page 209).

12 first-cut double-rib lamb chops
6 garlic cloves, cut into slivers
3 tablespoons lemon juice
¼ teaspoon ground cumin
salt
freshly ground black pepper
several drops sesame oil
watercress sprigs, for garnish

Remove all the fat from the lamb ribs, exposing the bones (you could ask the butcher to do this). Cover the bones with small pieces of aluminum foil. With the point of a sharp knife, make several incisions in each lamb chop and insert the garlic slivers.

In a small bowl, mix together the lemon juice, cumin, salt and black pepper to taste and the sesame oil.

Place the lamb chops in a deep bowl and pour the sauce over them. Marinate for 2 hours at room temperature.

Preheat the broiler for at least 30 minutes.

Broil the lamb chops on one side for 2 to 3 minutes for rare meat and longer for more well-done meat; turn the chops over and broil for 2 to 3 minutes longer.

Remove the aluminum foil from the chops; replace it with paper frills if desired. Arrange the chops on a serving platter and garnish with the watercress sprigs.

Poultry

Chicken

❧ Chicken-Stuffed ❧ Steamed Cabbage

Serves 6

This recipe was given to me by my Chinese friend Philip Li. He says that in Hong Kong, stuffed cabbage is eaten for Sunday brunch. I like it for dinner, served on a bed of steamed spinach.

1 head savoy cabbage
2 quarts water
1 ½ tablespoons black
  sesame seeds
1 tablespoon sesame oil
salt
freshly ground black pepper
3 whole chicken breasts,
  skinned and boned
1 bunch scallions, trimmed,
  but with green parts
12 thin slices kosher salami

½ cup Chicken Stock (see
  page 49)
2 tablespoons light soy
  sauce or low-sodium soy
  sauce
1 1-inch piece fresh ginger,
  grated, or 1 teaspoon
  dried ground ginger
2 tablespoons chopped
  parsley
Steamed Spinach with
  Garlic (see page 211)

With a sharp knife, remove and discard the core of the cabbage.

In a large saucepan, bring the water to a boil. Add the cabbage and bring the water back to a boil. Turn off the heat, cover and let stand 5 minutes. Drain and rinse under cold running water until the cabbage is cool. Drain well. Carefully separate the cabbage leaves. Reserve 12 large leaves and set them aside.

Chop the remaining cabbage leaves. Place them in a bowl and add the sesame seeds, ¼ teaspoon of the sesame oil and salt and black pepper to taste. Mix well and set aside.

Cut each chicken breast in half lengthwise. Cut each piece in half horizontally, to make 2 slices. Sprinkle the chicken with salt and black pepper to taste and a few drops of sesame oil. Set aside.

To stuff the cabbage leaves, on each leaf arrange a scallion; top with a slice of salami, then a slice of chicken breast, then some of the chopped cabbage. Roll up the cabbage leaf lengthwise to enclose the chicken, but leave the green end of the scallion sticking out (see illustration).

Place the cabbage rolls in a bamboo or metal steamer. Steam for 5 minutes or until the cabbage leaves are tender and the chicken is done.

In a small saucepan, heat the Chicken Stock. Add the remaining sesame oil (about ¼ teaspoon) and the soy sauce. Bring to a boil and turn off the heat. Add salt and black pepper to taste and the grated ginger and parsley.

Line a serving platter with the Steamed Spinach. Arrange the stuffed cabbage on top. Pour the sauce over the cabbage and serve.

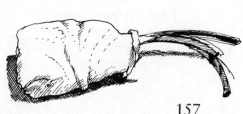

❦ Stuffed Roast Chicken ❦

Serves 6

3 tablespoons vegetable oil
½ teaspoon kosher salt
¼ teaspoon coarsely ground
   black pepper
1 cup coarsely chopped
   walnuts
2 chicken livers, coarsely
   chopped

1 chicken gizzard, coarsely
   chopped
2 scallions, thinly sliced
2 cups cooked rice
1 tablespoon dark soy sauce
   or low-sodium soy sauce
1 5-pound roasting chicken
1½ cups water

In a medium skillet, place 1 tablespoon of the oil and the kosher salt and coarsely ground pepper. Cook over high heat for 2 minutes, stirring constantly. Add the walnuts and cook for 2 minutes; add the livers and the gizzard and cook for 3 minutes more, stirring constantly. Remove from the heat.

Add the scallions and rice to the liver mixture. Mix well. Preheat the oven to 400°F.

Dry the chicken inside and out with paper towels. In a small bowl, mix together the remaining vegetable oil with the soy sauce. Rub the chicken inside and out with this mixture.

Stuff the cavity of the chicken with the liver-and-rice mixture. Cover the opening with aluminum foil. Place the chicken on a rack in a roasting pan and add the water. Bake for 1½ hours, or until the chicken is golden brown and the juices run clear when the thigh is pierced with a fork.

Remove the chicken from the oven and let it stand for 15 minutes before carving. Arrange the pieces of chicken on a serving platter, placing the stuffing in the center.

Pour the juice from the roasting pan into a sauceboat and serve along with the chicken.

❦ Chicken Liver Risotto ❦

Serves 4

3 tablespoons margarine
1 onion, chopped
1½ cups long-grain rice
2 cups boiling water
2 sprigs thyme or
    ½ teaspoon dried thyme
1 bay leaf
salt
freshly ground black pepper

2 tablespoons vegetable oil
1 pound chicken livers,
    trimmed
2 shallots, chopped
¾ cup dry white wine
½ cup Fresh Uncooked
    Tomato Coulis (see
    page 236)

Preheat the oven to 425°F.

In an ovenproof saucepan, melt 2 tablespoons of the margarine over low heat. Add the onion and cook for 2 minutes or just until transparent. Add the rice, raise the heat and cook, stirring, for 3 minutes more. Add the boiling water, thyme, bay leaf and salt and black pepper to taste. Mix well, remove from the heat, cover and bake for 20 minutes.

In a large skillet, heat the oil with the remaining margarine over high heat. Add the chicken livers, sprinkle with salt and black pepper and sauté until browned on all sides. Add the shallots, lower the heat and cook for 1 minute. Add the wine, raise the heat to high and cook until the wine is reduced by half. Add the Tomato Coulis, lower the heat, correct the seasoning and cook for 2 minutes longer. Remove from the heat.

Oil a 1½-quart Savarin mold.

Remove the rice from the oven. Remove the bay leaf and thyme sprigs. Put the rice into the mold, pushing it down with the back of a wooden spoon.

Unmold the rice onto a round serving platter. Fill the center hole with the chicken livers and the sauce (it will overflow onto the rice) and serve.

159

Chicken Sautéed with Limes

Serves 4

4 limes
6 tablespoons margarine
1 3½-pound chicken, cut into small pieces
1 onion, chopped
2 tablespoons all-purpose flour
2 cups Chicken Stock (see page 49)
½ silken bead curd cake, mashed
¼ teaspoon sesame oil
salt
freshly ground black pepper
¾ cup water
1 pound white mushroom caps, quartered

With a small, sharp knife, peel the zest from the limes, being careful not to include any of the white pith beneath the skin. Cut the zest into a julienne and set aside. Quarter each lime and dice each quarter. Set aside.

In a large saucepan, melt 4 tablespoons of the margarine over high heat. Add the chicken pieces and brown them on all sides. Add the onion and mix well. Sprinkle with the flour, mix again and cook for 2 minutes more. Add the Chicken Stock, stirring with a wooden spoon. Add the bean curd, sesame oil and salt and black pepper to taste. Mix again, cover, lower the heat and simmer for 30 minutes.

In another saucepan, place the diced limes; add the water and salt and black pepper to taste and bring to a boil. Add the mushrooms and cook over high heat for 5 minutes. Remove from the heat.

When the chicken is done, add the lime and mushroom mixture to the saucepan and cook for another 5 minutes. Remove from the heat.

To serve, place the chicken and the sauce in a deep serving bowl. Garnish with the julienned lime zest.

☙ Chicken with Saffron ☙

Serves 4

¼ cup olive oil
3 leeks, white parts only,
   thinly sliced
4 small onions, chopped
4 garlic cloves, chopped
1½ pounds ripe tomatoes,
   peeled, seeded and
   chopped
salt
freshly ground black pepper
½ teaspoon saffron, soaked
   in 1 teaspoon water

2 sprigs thyme or
   ½ teaspoon dried thyme
1 bay leaf
1 3½-pound chicken, cut
   into small pieces
1 tablespoon all-purpose
   flour
1 cup dry white wine
2 tablespoons chopped
   parsley

In a large saucepan, heat 2 tablespoons of the olive oil. Add the leeks, onions, garlic and tomatoes. Sprinkle with salt and black pepper to taste and add the saffron, thyme and bay leaf. Reduce the heat and simmer for 20 minutes, stirring occasionally. Remove from the heat and let cool.

Place the chicken in a large serving bowl and pour the leek and tomato mixture over it. Marinate for 1 hour.

One hour before serving, heat the remaining olive oil in a saucepan over high heat. Remove the chicken from the marinade (reserve the marinade) and brown the pieces on all sides. Remove the chicken from the saucepan and pour off the oil.

Return the chicken pieces to the saucepan, add the marinade and sprinkle with the flour. Mix well and add the wine. Bring to a boil, reduce the heat and simmer for 30 minutes.

Remove the chicken to a serving platter. Strain the sauce through a fine sieve over the chicken. Sprinkle with the chopped parsley and serve.

Roast Chicken
❦ with Mangoes and ❦
Straw Mushrooms

Serves 6

1 4-pound roasting chicken	1 tablespoon goose or
2 tablespoons dark soy	chicken fat
sauce or low-sodium soy	2 ripe mangoes, peeled,
sauce	pitted and thinly sliced
3 tablespoons lemon juice	½ cup dry white wine
salt	1 4-ounce can straw
freshly ground black pepper	mushrooms, drained
about 1½ cups Chicken	1 tablespoon chopped
Stock (see page 49)	parsley

Preheat the oven to 375°F.

Remove as much fat as possible from the chicken and reserve for another use. Rub the skin of the chicken with the soy sauce and place it in a roasting pan. Sprinkle it with 1½ tablespoons of the lemon juice and salt and black pepper to taste. Add the Chicken Stock to the roasting pan. Roast for 1 hour, basting from time to time. Add more Chicken Stock if necessary; there should always be about 1 cup of stock in the roasting pan.

In a large skillet, melt the goose fat over medium heat. Add the mango slices and sauté for 3 minutes. Add the white wine and simmer for 5 minutes. Add the mushrooms and cook until they are just heated through. Remove from the heat.

Carve the chicken and arrange the pieces in a circle on a serving platter. Place the mango slices in the center and pour the sauce with the mushrooms over the chicken. Sprinkle with the chopped parsley.

Chicken Sautéed with Peanuts

Serves 4

While we lived in Dodoma, a small town in the center of Tanzania where the new capital is to be built, this dish was taught to me by Mrs. Feruzi, my neighbor. All the ingredients can be found in any supermarket. Serve with boiled new potatoes.

3 tablespoons vegetable oil
1 3½-pound chicken, cut
   into serving pieces
2 onions, chopped
3 garlic cloves, chopped
2 large eggplants, cut into
   large cubes
1 tablespoon all-purpose
   flour
2 cups Chicken Stock (see
   page 49)

1 cup dry white wine
¼ pound shelled unsalted
   peanuts
2 bay leaves
1 sprig thyme or
   ½ teaspoon dried thyme
⅛ teaspoon cayenne pepper
salt
freshly ground black pepper

In a large saucepan, heat the oil over medium-high heat. Add the chicken pieces and brown them on all sides. Add the onions, garlic and eggplant and sauté for 3 minutes. Sprinkle with the flour, mix well and add the Chicken Stock and the wine. Bring to a boil and reduce the heat to medium. Add the peanuts, bay leaves, thyme, cayenne pepper and salt and black pepper to taste. Cook, covered, for 45 minutes or until the chicken is tender.

Remove the chicken pieces from the saucepan to a serving platter. Raise the heat and cook the sauce until it is reduced to 1 cup. Remove the bay leaves and thyme. Pour the sauce with the peanuts over the chicken and serve.

163

❧ Chickenburgers with ❧ Garlic Sauce

Serves 4

You can chop chicken with a food processor or a meat grinder. If you are using a food processor, cut the chicken breast in large cubes and, with the machine running, drop the pieces through the feed tube. Grind the chicken in two separate batches; if you don't, the bottom of the bowl will have puréed chicken instead of just finely chopped.

If you use a meat grinder, cut the chicken in long strips and use a fine blade. Trim off any membranes before grinding or the meat grinder may get stuck.

2 pounds chicken breasts, skinned, boned and chopped
3 scallions, finely chopped
1 egg
1 cake silken bean curd
salt
freshly ground black pepper
½ cup Teriyaki Sauce (see page 232)
4 tomatoes, sliced
1 large red onion, sliced
1 cup Garlic Sauce (see page 234)

Preheat the broiler.

In a large bowl, mix together the chicken, scallions, egg, bean curd and salt and black pepper to taste. Form the mixture into 4 patties.

Brush the chickenburgers on both sides with the Teriyaki Sauce. Broil for 6 minutes; with a spatula, turn the burgers over and broil for another 6 minutes.

Place the chickenburgers on a platter, garnish with the tomato and red onion slices, and serve with Garlic Sauce.

Chicken Livers with Port on Fresh Pasta

Serves 6

For this dish I like to use fresh tagliatelli, the 1/4-inch-wide flat egg pasta available in supermarkets and pasta stores.

6 tablespoons margarine
24 chicken livers (about
  2 pounds), trimmed
2 shallots, finely chopped
salt
freshly ground black pepper
1/3 cup Port wine
1/2 cup Vegetable Stock (see
  page 44)

1/4 pound shelled walnuts
1 pound fresh or dried egg
  or spinach tagliatelli
1 tablespoon vegetable oil
  (optional)
2 tablespoons chopped
  parsley

In a large skillet, melt the margarine over medim-high heat. Add the chicken livers and the shallots. Sauté until all sides of the livers are seared and the shallots are transparent but not browned. Sprinkle with salt and black pepper to taste. Add the Port and cook for 5 minutes. Lower the heat, add the Vegetable Stock and walnuts and simmer for 5 minutes more.

Bring a large pot of salted water to a boil. If using fresh pasta, add the oil. Add the pasta and cook for 5 minutes or until the pasta is *al dente*. Fresh pasta cooks very quickly; do not overcook. Drain well in a colander. (If using dried pasta, do not add oil to the water. Cook the pasta for 10 minutes or until the pasta is *al dente*.)

Place the pasta in a large serving bowl. Pour the chicken livers and the sauce over it. Sprinkle with the chopped parsley and serve.

165

❧ Stuffed Chicken ❧ Breasts

Serves 6

3 tablespoons olive oil
6 whole chicken breasts,
    boned, skin left on
salt
freshly ground black pepper
1 cup cooked wild rice
2 silken bean curd cakes
1 cup shelled hazelnuts,
chopped
2 shallots, chopped
2 tablespoons lime juice
2 cups Chicken Stock (see
    page 49)
1 tablespoon soy sauce or
    low-sodium soy sauce
4 scallions, finely chopped

Preheat the oven to 425°F.

In a large skillet, heat the oil over medium-high heat. Add the chicken breasts, skin-side down, and brown on both sides. Sprinkle with salt and black pepper to taste and remove to a platter to cool.

Place the wild rice in a mixing bowl. Add 1 bean curd cake, cubed, and the hazelnuts, shallots and salt and black pepper to taste. Add 1 tablespoon lime juice and toss gently with a wooden spoon.

Cut each chicken breast in half horizontally, to make 2 slices. Place some stuffing on the skinless side of a breast half. Cover with another breast half, skin-side up. With a spatula, place the stuffed chicken breast in a baking dish. Repeat with the remaining chicken breasts.

In a bowl, mix the Chicken Stock with the soy sauce; pour it over the chicken. Bake for 20 minutes.

Remove the baking dish from the oven. Arrange the stuffed chicken breasts on a serving platter and keep warm while preparing the sauce.

In a food processor, place the remaining bean curd cake, the cooking liquid from the baking dish and the remaining lime juice. Process until the sauce is thick and smooth. Pour into a bowl and add additional salt and black pepper to taste.

Sprinkle the chicken with the chopped scallions. Serve with the bean curd sauce in a sauceboat.

⚘ Sullivan Street ⚘ Fried Chicken

Serves 4

*F*ried chicken is not part of my childhood, but it is the *first American dish I had when I came to the United States some 25 years ago. I loved it then and I love it now. But, as with all the dishes I cook, I often change the recipes as I go along. This fried chicken is somewhat different from the first time I made it. In between, I discovered Chinese and Japanese ingredients; this recipe has been influenced by all the different cuisines I have learned to love. We live on Sullivan Street; so my children have always called this dish by our street's name.*

6 ounces mixed black and
  white sesame seeds
½ cup all-purpose flour
2 teaspoons paprika
2 teaspoons salt
1 3-pound chicken, cut into
  small serving pieces

1 egg
1 cup Chicken Stock (see
  page 49)
vegetable oil for frying
1 head Boston lettuce
5 scallions, trimmed and
  very finely chopped

167

Place the sesame seeds, flour, paprika and salt in a medium brown paper bag. Shake well. Add the chicken pieces and shake well again.

In a large bowl, beat together the egg and the Chicken Stock.

Dip each piece of coated chicken in the chicken stock mixture and place them on a platter. Return the chicken pieces to the brown paper bag and shake well again.

In a large deep-fryer or deep heavy skillet, put enough vegetable oil to cover half the chicken pieces; heat until it reaches about 360°F on a deep-frying thermometer. Add half the chicken pieces and cook until they are golden brown, about 6 to 8 minutes, turning them with metal tongs or a wire skimmer. Drain on paper towels and keep warm in a very low oven until all the chicken is fried.

Line a large platter with the Boston lettuce leaves. Place the chicken on top and sprinkle with the chopped scallions. Serve hot.

Roast Chicken ❦ with Shiitake ❦ Mushrooms

Serves 4 to 6

4 large dried shiitake
   mushrooms
1 cup water
1 6-pound roasting chicken
salt
freshly ground black pepper
1 tablespoon olive oil

2 tablespoons dark soy
   sauce or low-sodium soy
   sauce
2 cups Chicken Stock (see
   page 49)
parsley sprigs, for garnish

Soak the dried mushrooms in the water for at least
20 minutes.

Wipe the chicken inside and out with paper towels. With
your fingers, separate the breast skin from the meat.

Remove the mushrooms from the water, reserving the
soaking liquid. Cut off and discard the stems.

Preheat the oven to 425°F.

Slide the mushroom caps under the breast skin. Sprinkle
the chicken with salt and black pepper to taste; brush the
chicken with the olive oil.

Place the chicken in a large baking dish. Brush the
chicken with the soy sauce. Add the Chicken Stock and bake
for 45 minutes, basting from time to time. Add the reserved
mushroom liquid and bake for another 30 minutes, or until
the juices run clear when a thigh is pierced with a fork.

Remove the chicken from the baking dish and place it on
a large serving platter. Garnish the platter with parsley sprigs
and bring it to the table. (Carve either at the table or in the
kitchen.)

Pour the cooking liquids into a sauceboat and serve along
with the chicken.

To serve the chicken cold, let the chicken cool to room
temperature before refrigerating it. Pour the cooking liquids
into a large bowl and refrigerate. When ready to use, remove
the fat which has risen to the top of the cooking liquids. Use
the remaining set chicken jelly as a garnish for the cold roast
chicken.

169

Chicken Sautéed with
☙ Artichoke Hearts ☙
and Pears

Serves 4

*T*his dish is excellent served with lightly sautéed snow
peas.

2 tablespoons vegetable oil
1 3½-pound chicken, cut
   into serving pieces
salt
freshly ground black pepper
1 pound small onions
1 teaspoon paprika
1½ cups Chicken Stock (see
   page 49)

⅓ cup wine vinegar
4 pears
1 tablespoon lemon juice
1 16-ounce can artichoke
   hearts, drained
parsley sprigs, for garnish

In a large saucepan, heat the oil over medium-high heat. Add
the chicken pieces, sprinkle with salt and black pepper to
taste and brown on all sides. Remove the chicken to a platter.
   Add the onions to the saucepan and sauté over medium
heat until light brown. Add the chicken pieces. Sprinkle with
the paprika, mix well and add the Chicken Stock and
vinegar. Bring to a boil, lower the heat and simmer, covered,
for 40 minutes.
   Peel and core the pears. With a melon-baller, make as
many pear balls as possible. Toss them with the lemon juice
and set aside.
   Just before serving, add the artichoke hearts and pear
balls to the saucepan. Cook until they are just heated
through. Remove the chicken to a platter. Arrange the

onions, artichoke hearts and pear balls around the chicken. Strain the sauce through a fine sieve placed over a bowl. Pour the sauce over the chicken. Garnish with parsley sprigs and serve.

Chicken Fricassee with Sorrel Sauce

Serves 4

½ pound sorrel
2 tablespoons vegetable oil
1 3-pound chicken, cut into
   serving pieces
salt
freshly ground black pepper

2 tablespoons chicken fat
2 onions, sliced
1 tablespoon all-purpose
   flour
4 cups Chicken Stock (see
   page 49)

Wash the sorrel and cut off the tough stems. Drain well and pat dry with paper towels.

In a large deep skillet, heat the oil over high heat. Add half the chicken pieces and sauté until browned on all sides; sprinkle with salt and black pepper to taste. Remove the chicken pieces to a platter and brown the remaining chicken. Keep the chicken pieces warm in a 200°F oven.

Pour off the oil from the skillet. Add the chicken fat and heat until it melts. Add the onions and cook over medium heat until they are transparent. Sprinkle the onions with the flour and mix well. Add the Chicken Stock and salt and black pepper to taste. Add the sorrel and the chicken pieces. Simmer over medium heat for about 20 minutes, or until the chicken is easily pierced with a fork.

Remove the chicken pieces to a serving platter. Pour the sauce in the skillet over the chicken and serve.

Chicken with Two Kinds of Celery

Serves 4

1 large head celery
1 large celery root, about
   1 pound, peeled and cut
   into ½-inch dice
2 large baking potatoes,
   peeled and cut into
   ½-inch dice
1 cup Chicken Stock (see
   page 49)
salt

freshly ground black pepper
2 tablespoons vegetable oil
2 whole chicken breasts,
   skinned, boned and
   diced
1 tablespoon sugar
1 tablespoon lemon juice
¼ teaspoon sesame oil
1 hot red pimento, sliced
½ cup water

Remove the tough green outer celery stalks and set them aside for another use. Trim the celery heart; set the leaves aside for garnish. Thinly slice the pale yellow inner celery stalks.

In a large saucepan, place all the vegetables and add the Chicken Stock. Bring to a boil, reduce the heat and simmer, covered, for 10 minutes or until the vegetables are tender and the stock is all absorbed. Add salt and black pepper to taste.

In a medium skillet, heat the oil over high heat. Add the chicken and sprinkle it with the sugar and lemon juice. Sauté until browned on all sides. Add the sesame oil, the hot pimento, salt and black pepper to taste; then cook for 5 minutes. Add the vegetables and the water and cook over medium heat, uncovered, for 3 minutes longer.

Remove from the heat and arrange on a serving platter. Garnish with the celery leaves and serve.

៥ Chicken Paillardes ៥

Serves 4

*P*aillarde in French means a very thin slice of meat or
poultry, broiled quickly over very high heat. This recipe
is very simple and takes about 5 minutes to cook. The
chicken can be replaced by very thin slices of beef cut from
the round or sirloin.

2 whole chicken breasts,
  skinned and boned
2 tablespoons light soy
  sauce or low-sodium soy
  sauce
2 garlic cloves, finely
  chopped

salt
freshly ground black pepper
2 tablespoons lime juice
1 lime, thinly sliced
parsley sprigs, for garnish

Cut each breast in half lengthwise; then cut each half in half
again (see illustration). Place each piece between two sheets
of waxed paper and pound with a mallet or the bottom of a
skillet until the slices are flattened and about ⅛ inch thick.

Mix the soy sauce with the garlic in a small bowl. Place
the chicken paillardes on a serving platter and pour the soy
sauce mixture over them. Rub the sauce into the chicken
with your fingers and marinate for 10 minutes.

Preheat the broiler to high.

Arrange the paillardes in a broiling pan. Broil for
2 minutes; turn and broil for another 2 minutes. Place the
paillardes on a serving platter.
Sprinkle them with salt and
black pepper to taste. Sprinkle
a few drops of lime juice over
each paillarde and top each
with a lime slice. Garnish with
parsley sprigs and serve.

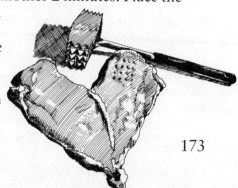

173

🫖 Chicken and Rice 🫖 in Lemon Sauce

Serves 4

I spent my early childhood in Cairo in a large house filled *with children of all ages, grandmothers, aunts and Fatima. Fatima was the person in charge of me! She was about two years older than me. Her mother was my grandmother's cook—and what a great cook she was. Our favorite pastime was to stay in the kitchen, tasting whatever Fatima's mother was preparing. Our favorite day was when my grandmother went to her sister's house for dinner. That day we would have boiled chicken topped with a rich lemon sauce and rice. I haven't seen Fatima in 30 years and I don't know what happened to her, but whenever I make this dish, I smile at the memory of two little girls licking wooden spoons in a warm kitchen.*

1 3½-pound chicken	salt
1½ quarts Chicken Stock	2 eggs
(see page 49)	6 tablespoons lemon juice
2½ cups water	freshly ground black pepper
2 cups long-grain rice	

Remove as much fat as possible from the chicken. Set the fat aside.

Place the chicken in a large saucepan. Add the Chicken Stock, bring to a boil, reduce the heat and simmer for 45 minutes or until the juices from a thigh run clear when it is pierced with a fork. Remove the chicken to a platter and keep warm in a very low oven; reserve the stock.

Cut the chicken fat into small pieces. In a small saucepan, melt the fat over very low heat. Strain the fat through a very fine sieve. Set aside.

174

In another saucepan, bring the water to a boil. Add the rice, 1 tablespoon of the clarified chicken fat and salt to taste. Bring to a boil again, lower the heat, cover and simmer for 15 minutes. Fluff the rice with a fork and cook, uncovered, over low heat for another 15 minutes or until the rice is tender and all the liquid is gone; add more water if necessary.

In a mixing bowl, beat the eggs with a fork. While still beating, add 2 cups of the chicken stock and the lemon juice. Pour the liquid into a medium saucepan, add salt and black pepper to taste and cook over low heat, stirring constantly, until the sauce thickens; do not let it boil or the sauce will curdle. Set aside.

Carve the chicken into 6 to 8 serving pieces.

Place the rice in a deep serving bowl. Arrange the chicken pieces on top. Pour half the sauce over the chicken and serve the remaining sauce in a sauceboat.

❦ Stuffed Chicken Breasts ❦ with Cucumbers

Serves 4

2 chicken thighs, skinned and boned
2 chicken legs, skinned and boned
4 egg whites
2 cakes silken bean curd
½ pound white mushrooms, trimmed and sliced
1 tablespoon dried tarragon
salt
freshly ground black pepper

2 whole chicken breasts, boned
2 eggs
1 cup plain breadcrumbs
2 pounds cucumbers
4 tablespoons vegetable oil
1 pound fresh peas
1 cup dry white wine
⅛ teaspoon nutmeg
2 tablespoons chopped parsley

175

Cut the meat from the thighs and legs into small pieces. Place this meat, the egg whites, 1 bean curd cake and the mushrooms in a food processor. Process until the ingredients are finely chopped. Put the mixture in a large bowl. Add the tarragon and salt and black pepper to taste. Refrigerate the stuffing for 1 hour.

Cut each chicken breast in half lengthwise. Cut each half in half horizontally, to make 2 slices. Spread the stuffing on one side of each half-breast slice. Cover the stuffing with the other slice. Set aside.

Beat the eggs in a large bowl. Spread the breadcrumbs on a large plate. Carefully dip the stuffed chicken breasts in the eggs, then carefully dredge them with the breadcrumbs. Place them side-by-side on a serving platter and refrigerate while preparing the cucumbers.

Peel and trim the cucumbers. Cut each cucumber in half lengthwise and remove the seeds with a spoon. Cut the cucumber halves into 2-inch pieces and trim them to look like very large olives.

Place the cucumbers in a large saucepan, add enough boiling water to cover and cook over medium heat for 1 minute. Drain the cucumbers and rinse them well with cold water.

Beat the remaining bean curd cake in a bowl with a fork, until smooth.

In a large skillet, heat the oil over high heat. Add the stuffed chicken breasts and sauté for 5 minutes; turn them over and cook for 5 minutes longer. Carefully place the chicken on a heated platter.

Add the cucumbers and the peas to the skillet along with the bean curd and the wine. Bring to a boil and then lower the heat; add the nutmeg and salt and black pepper to taste and simmer for 10 minutes.

To serve, surround the stuffed chicken with the cucumbers and peas. Sprinkle the chopped parsley on top.

Roast Chicken with Miniature Bananas

Serves 4

I developed this recipe after I received a case of tiny bananas from Florida. These bananas, the size of a fat thumb, were once grown only in Central and South America, but now they are grown in Florida; the grower wanted me to be the first to taste them. A case of bananas, however small they are, is a lot of bananas! For weeks we ate them for breakfast, lunch and dinner. We ate them broiled, sautéed in butter, with broiled chicken, with fish—with everything. Of all the recipes I came up with, this is my favorite. Pieces of chicken are rolled in breadcrumbs and roasted along with the bananas. The crisp chicken goes well with the tender sweet bananas. You need an ovenproof serving dish, the tiny bananas (now available in many supermarkets) and an open mind to enjoy this dish.

2 eggs
salt
freshly ground black pepper
4 tablespoons all-purpose
  flour
6 tablespoons fine plain
  breadcrumbs
1 3½-pound chicken, cut
  into serving pieces
3 tablespoons olive oil

12 tiny bananas, or
  3 regular bananas cut in
  thirds
3 tablespoons lemon juice
½ teaspoon cinnamon
⅛ teaspoon nutmeg
4 tablespoons margarine,
  cut into small pieces
parsley sprigs, for garnish

Preheat the oven to 425°F.

In a shallow bowl, beat the eggs with salt and black pepper to taste.

In another shallow bowl, spread the flour; in a third bowl, spread the breadcrumbs.

177

Roll each piece of chicken first in the flour, then in the egg and finally in the breadcrumbs.

Arrange the chicken pieces in one layer in an ovenproof serving dish. Sprinkle with salt and black pepper to taste. Drizzle the olive oil over the chicken and bake 20 minutes.

Peel the bananas and sprinkle them with some of the lemon juice.

Turn the chicken pieces over and cook for another 10 minutes. Add the bananas and sprinkle them with the remaining lemon juice and the cinnamon and nutmeg. Dot the chicken and the bananas with the margarine. Bake for another 10 minutes, basting with the pan juices; add ¼ cup water if there is not enough liquid.

Remove the dish from the oven and serve immediately, garnished with the parsley sprigs.

Chicken Breasts
❧ Sautéed with ❧
Garlic Cloves

Serves 4

The idea of this recipe is to roast the whole garlic heads and then add the chicken breasts to the roasting pan. When serving the garlic, tell your guests to mash the roast garlic out of its skin with a fork. Roast garlic is very mild. Serve this dish with a purée of broccoli or cauliflower.

4 whole garlic heads
2 tablespoons olive oil
1 cup dry white wine
4 whole chicken breasts,
  boned and halved
salt

freshly ground black pepper
2 tablespoons soy sauce or
  low-sodium soy sauce
½ cup Chicken Stock (see
  page 49)

Preheat the oven to 375°F.

Cut a shallow circle around each garlic head, about 1 inch from the top, and remove the outer skin.

Place the heads of garlic in a roasting pan and brush them with the olive oil. Add the white wine, cover the pan with aluminum foil and bake for 45 minutes.

Remove the aluminum foil and arrange the chicken breasts around the garlic, skin-side up. Sprinkle the chicken breasts with salt and black pepper to taste and brush them with the soy sauce.

Raise the oven temperature to 425°F and bake for 15 minutes.

Remove the chicken breasts to a serving platter. Arrange the garlic heads around the chicken.

Add the Chicken Stock to the roasting pan. Place the pan on the stove top over high heat and bring to a boil, scraping the sides and bottom to dissolve the pan deposits. Add more black pepper if desired. Pour the sauce over the chicken and serve.

Poached Chicken with Broccoli

Serves 6

4 cups Chicken Stock (see
  page 49)
6 whole chicken breasts,
  skinned, boned and
  halved
2 teaspoons dried tarragon
  or 2 tablespoons
  chopped fresh tarragon
1 head broccoli

2 tablespoons margarine
2 tablespoons all-purpose
  flour
salt
freshly ground black pepper
3 teaspoons dry sherry
¼ cup plain breadcrumbs

In a large saucepan, bring the Chicken Stock to a boil.
Reduce the heat and add the chicken breast halves. Simmer
for 10 minutes. With a slotted spoon, remove the chicken
breasts and cut them into serving pieces. Place the pieces on a
plate and sprinkle with the tarragon. Set aside and keep
warm.

Measure out 2 cups of the chicken broth and set aside.
Refrigerate the remaining broth for another use.

Preheat the oven to 425°F.

Trim off the tough stems of the broccoli and separate the
head into florets. (The stems can be used for making broccoli
soup with the remaining chicken stock.) Steam the florets in a
bamboo or metal steamer for 5 minutes or until they are just
tender. Remove from the heat and set aside.

In a small saucepan, melt the margarine over medium
heat. Add the flour and mix well, slowly add the reserved
chicken broth, stirring constantly with a wooden spoon. Add
salt and black pepper to taste and the sherry. Simmer for
5 minutes over very low heat. The sauce should be very
smooth; if it is not, pour it into a blender and blend for
5 seconds. Remove from the heat.

180

Line a large ovenproof serving dish with the broccoli florets. Sprinkle with salt and black pepper to taste. Add the sliced chicken. Pour the sauce over the chicken and sprinkle the breadcrumbs on top. Bake for 12 minutes or until nicely browned on top. Serve immediately.

❧ Liver Knishes ❧

Serves 6

*T*he avocado should be peeled, sliced thinly lengthwise and then sprinkled with lemon juice to prevent discoloration while preparing the potatoes.

1 pound potatoes, boiled
  and peeled
1 egg
salt
freshly ground black pepper
about 2 tablespoons matzo
  meal
2 tablespoons olive oil
1 large onion, diced
½ pound chicken livers

1 tablespoon brandy
1 teaspoon dried tarragon
1 teaspoon vegetable oil
2 avocados, peeled, thinly
  sliced and tossed with
  1 teaspoon lemon juice
1 pound Belgian endives,
  leaves separated
½ cup Classic Vinaigrette
  (see page 230)

In a large bowl, mash the potatoes with a fork or a ricer. Add the egg and salt and black pepper to taste. Mix well with a wooden spoon. Add the matzo meal and mix well. Add more matzo meal if necessary to form a purée firm enough to be molded.

In a medium skillet, heat the olive oil over medium heat. Add the onion and sauté until light brown. Add the chicken livers; raise the heat and sauté until the livers are browned on all sides but still pink inside. Add the brandy and carefully

181

ignite it with a match. When the flames die down, sprinkle the livers with salt and black pepper to taste and the tarragon. With a spatula, transfer the livers and onions to a plate to cool. Coarsely chop the livers and set aside.

Preheat the oven to 400°F.

Form small balls about 1 inch in diameter with the potato purée. With your finger, make a hole in the center of each ball and insert some of the chicken livers and onions. Close the holes and flatten the balls into disks about ¼ inch thick.

Grease a baking sheet with the vegetable oil. Place the knishes on the sheet and bake until they are golden brown.

On each individual serving plate, arrange alternate slices of avocado and endive leaves in a circle, forming a daisy pattern. In the center, place 2 or 3 knishes. Pour some Vinaigrette over the salad and serve.

Turkey

Thanksgiving
❦ Stuffed Turkey with ❦
Fruit and Nut Stuffing

Serves 15

Here's one way to ensure a delicious, moist turkey: marinate it in the refrigerator for three days before cooking and slide some shiitake mushrooms under the breast skin before it goes into the oven. Serve the turkey with kale and cranberries.

1 20-pound fresh turkey

Marinade:

4 cups dry white wine
4 tablespoons lime juice
3 tablespoons lemon juice
10 garlic cloves, chopped
4 onions, chopped

1 tablespoon dried oregano
1 teaspoon chopped red or
  green pimento
salt
freshly ground black pepper

10 shiitake mushrooms,
  soaked overnight in
  enough water to cover

4 tablespoons margarine
3 tablespoons dark soy
  sauce or low-sodium soy
  sauce

Stuffing:

1 turkey liver
1 turkey gizzard
7 ounces coarse plain
  breadcrumbs
½ pound dried apricots,
  quartered
3 Granny Smith apples,
  peeled, cored and diced
2 eggs, beaten
2 garlic cloves, chopped

2 sprigs fresh marjoram,
  chopped
1 cup shelled walnuts,
  coarsely chopped
1 cup shelled unsalted
  pistachio nuts
1 cup Chicken Stock (see
  page 49)
salt
freshly ground black pepper

4 cups Chicken Stock

Dry the turkey inside and out with paper towels. Cut off the neck but keep the skin intact (some of the stuffing will fill the neck part). Place the turkey in a large roasting pan.

In a large bowl, mix together all the marinade ingredients. Pour the marinade over the turkey; spoon some into the turkey's cavity. Cover the turkey and pan with aluminum foil and refrigerate for 3 days, turning the turkey from time to time.

183

On the day the turkey will be served, drain the mushrooms. Cut off and discard the stems.

Remove the turkey from the marinade; do not remove the marinade from the roasting pan. With your fingers, separate the breast skin from the meat. Insert 2 mushroom caps and 1 tablespoon of margarine under the skin on each side. Sprinkle the turkey with black pepper and rub the skin all over with soy sauce.

For the stuffing, coarsely chop the turkey liver, gizzard and the remaining shiitake mushrooms. Place in a large mixing bowl. Add all the stuffing ingredients and mix well.

Preheat the oven to 350°F.

Fill the turkey's cavity with the stuffing. Do not overstuff, because the stuffing will expand as it cooks. Close the cavity with wooden toothpicks. Place some stuffing under the turkey's skin at the neck and close the skin with wooden toothpicks. If any stuffing remains, place it on a piece of aluminum foil, roll it up like a sausage, and twist the ends closed. Place the turkey back in the roasting pan; place the package alongside it.

Add the 4 cups of Chicken Stock to the marinade. Dot the turkey breast with the remaining margarine and bake, loosely covered with aluminum foil, for 5½ hours, basting from time to time.

Remove from the oven. Let the turkey stand for 15 minutes in its own juices before carving.

Strain the pan liquids through a very fine sieve placed over a saucepan. Heat the sauce but do not let it boil. Serve with the turkey and stuffing.

Turkey Scaloppine with Paprika

Serves 6

*S*erve plain rice or a simple fresh pasta with this dish.

2 pounds boneless turkey breast	3 tablespoons olive oil
4 tablespoons all-purpose flour	1 teaspoon paprika
1 tablespoon dried oregano	1 6-ounce jar marinated artichoke hearts, drained
salt	2 cups Sweet Red Pepper Sauce (see page 235)
freshly ground black pepper	parsley sprigs, for garnish

Thinly slice the turkey breast. Place the slices between sheets of waxed paper. With a mallet or the back of a heavy skillet, pound the slices until they are very thin.

Combine the flour in a dish with the oregano and salt and black pepper to taste. Lightly dredge the turkey slices with the mixture.

In a large skillet, heat the oil over high heat. When it is very hot, add the turkey slices and cook until they are browned on both sides. Sprinkle the slices with the paprika, reduce the heat and cook 5 minutes longer. Add the artichokes and cook until they are heated enough.

Arrange the turkey slices on a large serving platter and surround them with the artichokes. Pour some of the Sweet Red Pepper Sauce over the slices and garnish with the parsley. Serve the remaining sauce in a sauceboat on the side.

❧ Braised Boned ❧ Turkey Breast

Serves 6

*T*urkey is not just for Thanksgiving. Boned turkey breast, which is excellent braised with onions and endives, is available year-round in any supermarket.

1 3-pound boned turkey
   breast
2 tablespoons all-purpose
   flour
3 tablespoons olive oil
2 large onions, sliced
2 garlic cloves, finely
   chopped
3 cups Chicken Stock (see
   page 49)

2 tablespoons dark soy
   sauce or low-sodium soy
   sauce
1 sprig thyme or
   ½ teaspoon dried thyme
salt
freshly ground black pepper
2 heads Boston lettuce
6 Belgian endives
1 tablespoon sugar
1½ tablespoons lemon juice

Dust the turkey breast all over with the flour.

In a large casserole, heat the oil over high heat. Add the onions, reduce the heat and sauté until the onions are transparent; add the garlic and the turkey breast. Raise the heat and brown the breast on all sides.

In a bowl, mix the Chicken Stock with the soy sauce. Add them to the casserole. Add the thyme and salt and black pepper to taste. Bring to a boil again, reduce the heat, cover and simmer for 1 hour.

Cut each Boston lettuce in half. Wash each half and pat dry with paper towels. Tie each lettuce half around the center with a piece of kitchen string. Add them to the casserole.

Wipe the endives and add them to the casserole. Sprinkle the lettuce halves and endives with the sugar. Raise the heat to medium and cook for 10 minutes. Add the lemon juice and cook for 10 minutes more.

Remove the turkey breast to a cutting board. Let it stand 5 minutes before slicing. Arrange the slices on a serving platter.

Remove the lettuce from the casserole. Cut off the strings and arrange the lettuce around the turkey. Remove the endives and place them between the lettuce portions.

Heat the sauce in the casserole on the stovetop and pour some over the turkey slices. Serve the remaining sauce in a sauceboat.

Cornish Hens

Broiled Marinated Cornish Hens

Serves 6

6 Cornish hens
4 tablespoons olive oil
3 tablespoons lemon juice
1 tablespoon balsamic
    vinegar
¼ teaspoon ground cumin
1 garlic clove, crushed

salt
freshly ground black pepper
watercress sprigs, for
    garnish
½ cup Green Sauce (see
    page 242)

With a sharp heavy knife, split each Cornish hen in half along the backbone (you could ask the butcher to do this). Flatten them.

187

In a bowl large enough to hold all the Cornish hens, mix together the olive oil, lemon juice, vinegar, cumin, garlic and salt and black pepper to taste. Roll the Cornish hens, one by one, in the marinade and let stand for 2 hours.

Preheat the broiler until it is very hot. Place the Cornish hens, breast-side-down, on a large broiling pan and broil for 5 minutes. Turn the hens over and broil for 10 minutes longer, basting from time to time with the marinade.

Arrange the hens on a large platter, garnish with watercress sprigs and serve with Green Sauce.

Cornish Hens with Lima Beans

Serves 4

*F*resh lima beans in late summer are sweet as can be and very tender. This dish can be made in advance and kept warm in the steamer or served cold.

4 Cornish hens
2 tablespoons dark soy
    sauce or low-sodium soy
    sauce
1 cup water
1 head Boston lettuce
2 pounds fresh or 2
    10-ounce boxes frozen
    lima beans

3 sprigs fresh sage or
    1 teaspoon dried sage
3 tablespoons olive oil
2 tablespoons lemon juice
salt
freshly ground black pepper

Preheat the oven to 425°F.

Rub the skins of the Cornish hens with the soy sauce. Place them on a rack in a baking pan; add the water and bake for 40 minutes, or until the juices run clear when a thigh is pricked with a fork.

If serving hot, set the hens aside to keep warm. If serving cold, let the hens cool to room temperature in their own juices.

Line a bamboo or metal steamer with the lettuce leaves. Place the lima beans and 2 sprigs of the sage on top, cover and steam for about 10 minutes for fresh lima beans (5 minutes for frozen), until tender.

In a small bowl, combine the olive oil, lemon juice and salt and black pepper to taste. Chop the remaining sage sprig and add it to the bowl. Mix well with a wire whisk.

To serve hot, cut the Cornish hens into small pieces with kitchen shears. Add them to the cooked lima beans. Toss gently with a fork, trying not to tear the lettuce below.

Place a large serving platter on top of the steamer basket. Invert basket and platter together and lift off the basket. With a knife, cut an X in the center of the lettuce leaves and fold them back. Pour the lemon dressing over the dish and serve.

To serve cold, remove the lima beans to a serving bowl. Cut the Cornish hens into small pieces with kitchen shears and add them to the beans. Cover and refrigerate until ready to serve. Refrigerate the sauce from the roasting pan in a separate bowl. Just before serving, pour the lemon sauce over the lima beans and chicken and toss. The juice from the roasting pan will be jellied; garnish with the jelly and serve.

Cornish Hens with Lemons

Serves 4

4 Cornish hens
3 lemons
3 tablespoons soy sauce or low-sodium soy sauce
3 tablespoons lemon juice
salt
freshly ground black pepper
1 cup water

2 pounds medium onions, coarsely chopped
4 cups Chicken Stock (see page 49)
1 teaspoon whole coriander seeds
parsley sprigs, for garnish

Preheat the oven to 375°F.

With a sharp, heavy knife, split each Cornish hen in half along the backbone (you could ask your butcher to do this).

Cut 1 lemon in half and rub the Cornish hens with it inside and out. Thinly slice the remaining lemons.

In a small bowl, combine the soy sauce and the lemon juice.

Place the Cornish hens in a baking pan, skin-side up. Brush with the soy sauce mixture and sprinkle with salt and black pepper to taste. Add the water to the baking pan. Bake for 40 minutes or until the juices run clear when a thigh is pricked with a fork.

In a medium saucepan, place the onions and the lemon slices, Chicken Stock, coriander and salt and black pepper to taste. Bring to a boil, lower the heat, cover and simmer for 45 minutes, stirring occasionally.

With a slotted spoon, remove the onions and lemon slices from the stock. Arrange them on a serving platter and top with the roasted Cornish hens. Garnish with parsley sprigs and serve.

Duck and Goose

❦ Roast Duck ❦
with Pears

Serves 8

A Chinese friend once told me that the best way to prepare a duck is to stuff it with paper towels and refrigerate it for 2 days, uncovered. The reason, he explained, is that this dries the skin; when the skin is pricked before cooking, the fat runs out and the skin turns crisp. I tried this method and found that my duck or goose was free of fat and its skin was always delicately brown and crisp.

In exchange for his tip, I gave my friend one of mine: Cut off the neck skin, sew it to form a pouch, stuff it with chopped veal and duck livers and cook it alongside the duck. The stuffed neck makes a wonderful pâté the next day, served in thin slices with an endive salad.

The ducks in this recipe should be roasted in a large baking dish, one big enough to hold them along with the necks and pears. Use tiny Seckel pears, available in the fall. Serve the ducks with noodles, rice, or a lentil purée.

2 3- to 3½-pound ducks
2 pounds Seckel pears
3 tablespoons lemon juice
½ cup sake or dry white
  wine
4 garlic cloves, cut into
  eighths

salt
freshly ground black pepper
4 tablespoons dark soy
  sauce or low-sodium soy
  sauce
3 cups water

191

Neck Stuffing:

1 pound chopped veal	salt
2 duck livers, cut into small pieces	freshly ground black pepper
2 eggs	4 tablespoons all-purpose flour
1 garlic clove, chopped	

Wipe the ducks with paper towels. Remove as much fat as possible. Cut off the neck skins and reserve them. Fill the duck cavities with clean paper towels. Refrigerate, uncovered, overnight.

Peel the pears, but leave on the little stems. Combine the lemon juice and sake in a large bowl. Soak the pears in the mixture for 2 hours before cooking the ducks.

Preheat the oven to 425°F.

With the tip of a sharp knife, make slits in the duck breasts, thighs and sides and insert slivers of garlic. Prick the duck skins all over with a fork to allow the fat to flow freely. Rub the ducks with salt and black pepper to taste.

Place the ducks in a large baking dish and brush them with the soy sauce. Add the water to the dish and bake for 2 hours, basting from time to time.

As soon as the ducks go into the oven, prepare the stuffed necks. Using a heavy needle and heavy white cotton thread, sew the duck necks into pouches, starting with the narrow end (see illustration). Leave an opening big enough to add the stuffing.

In a large bowl, mix together the veal, duck livers, eggs and garlic. Add salt and black pepper to taste. Add the flour and mix again.

Pack the duck necks with the stuffing and sew the openings closed. Add the necks to the baking dish after the ducks have been in the oven for 1 hour. Cook for 1 hour, until the ducks are done.

Forty-five minutes before the ducks are ready, add the pears with their liquid to the baking dish. Baste from time to time.

To serve, cut each duck into quarters. Arrange the pieces on a serving platter and surround them with the pears.

Cool the stuffed necks to room temperature. Wrap them in aluminum foil and refrigerate overnight.

Pour the liquid from the baking dish into a large mixing bowl. Using the ladle, skim off all the fat from the surface. (Pour the fat into a plastic container and refrigerate for later use.) Pour the sauce into a sauceboat and serve with the ducks.

Roast Goose with Apples

Serves 6

One of the reasons I like to roast a goose is for its fat. Nothing is more wonderful than potatoes or chicken livers sautéed in goose fat. To render goose fat, pull out as much of it as you can from inside the goose. Dice the fat and cook it over low heat until it is liquid, with little golden brown, crisp cracklings. Strain the goose fat, pour it into plastic containers and store in the refrigerator. The goose fat will keep for several months. As for the delicious cracklings, just sprinkle them with kosher salt and serve hot on slices of fresh rye bread with drinks. But beware of calories!

1 8-pound goose
1 tablespoon kosher salt
freshly ground black pepper
1 cup water
about 2 cups Chicken Stock
    (see page 49)

6 Granny Smith apples
2 cups white wine
4 tablespoons sugar
¼ teaspoon cinnamon

Preheat the oven to 425°F.

Remove all the loose fat from the goose and set it aside for another use. Prick the skin of the goose all over with a fork. In a small bowl, combine the salt and black pepper to taste and rub the goose inside and out with the mixture.

Place the goose on a rack in a baking dish. Add the water to the dish and bake for 15 minutes. Remove the goose from the oven and pour the goose fat in the pan into a bowl; set it aside for another use. Add 2 cups of Chicken Stock to the baking pan. Reduce the oven temperature to 350°F and bake the goose for 2 hours longer, basting from time to time. Add more Chicken Stock if needed.

Peel the apples. Cut them in half lengthwise and core them. Arrange the apples side by side in a large skillet, cut-sides down. Pour the wine over the apples. Add the sugar and cinnamon and sprinkle with black pepper to taste. Bring to a boil, reduce the heat and simmer for 25 minutes. With a slotted spatula, remove 6 apple halves; set them aside in a warm place. Purée the remaining apples and their liquid in a food processor. Pour the purée into a bowl.

Remove the goose from the oven and let it stand for 10 minutes. Carve the goose and arrange the pieces on a serving platter. Surround with the reserved apple halves.

Pour the pan juices into a bowl and skim off the fat. Pour the juices back into the baking pan and add the apple purée and some Chicken Stock if needed—the sauce should not be too thick. Mix well and heat gently on the stove top. Pour some of the sauce over the apples and serve the rest in a sauceboat with the goose.

ଏ Mrs. Chino's Duck ଏ with Beets

Serves 4

I discovered how wonderful beets are when traveling in California to research new vegetables. After I interviewed one grower, he suggested I stay for dinner. His mother made duck with tiny, tender, very sweet beets, served with a superb sauce. When I asked what made it so special, she told me it included beet leaves. Just before I left San Diego, she gave me a basket of miniature vegetables to take home, along with the recipe for her duck. Serve this with plain rice or mashed potatoes.

3 tablespoons duck fat, chopped
1 3⅓-pound duck, cut into small serving pieces
2 shallots, chopped
2 cups Chicken Stock (see page 49)
1 cup sake or white wine
3 tablespoons chopped fresh sage or 2 teaspoons dried sage

⅛ teaspoon nutmeg
2 bay leaves
2 garlic cloves, crushed
salt
freshly ground black pepper
3 pounds baby beets, with stems and leaves
3 tablespoons lemon juice
watercress sprigs, for garnish

In a large saucepan, melt the chopped duck fat over medium heat and cook until the fat is rendered. With a slotted spatula, remove any unmelted solids from the duck fat and discard. Add the duck pieces and the shallots. Raise the heat to high and brown the duck on all sides. Add the Chicken Stock, sake, sage, nutmeg, bay leaves, garlic and salt and black pepper to taste. Bring to a boil, reduce the heat and cook over medium heat, uncovered, for 40 minutes.

195

Peel the beets, leaving on the leaves. Place the beets in a bamboo or metal steamer and steam for 10 minutes, or until the beets are tender.

Arrange the duck pieces on a serving platter and keep warm.

Cut off and reserve the leaves from the beets. Arrange the beets around the duck.

Pour the liquid from the saucepan into a bowl. The fat will rise to the surface; with a ladle, remove as much of the fat as you can.

Place the beet leaves and the duck liquid in a food processor. Process until puréed. Pour the sauce over the duck.

Duck with Red Cabbage

Serves 4

1 3½-pound duck
2 garlic cloves, quartered
salt
freshly ground black pepper
1 head red cabbage, about
    3 pounds
½ cup wine vinegar
4 Granny Smith apples,
    peeled, cored and sliced

1 tablespoon honey
1 tablespoon chopped fresh
    thyme or 1 teaspoon
    dried thyme
1 tablespoon black sesame
    seeds
¼ teaspoon sesame oil

Preheat the oven to 375°F.

Dry the duck inside and out with paper towels. With the tip of a small sharp knife, make slits in the duck breast and insert the garlic quarters. Sprinkle the skin with salt and black pepper to taste. Prick the skin of the duck all over with a fork. Put the duck in a baking dish and bake for 1½ hours. Remove from the oven and keep warm.

Trim and quarter the red cabbage. Remove and discard the central core and julienne the cabbage.

In a large saucepan, place the cabbage and cover it with cold water; add 1 tablespoon of the vinegar to the water. Bring to a boil and cook for 1 minute. Remove from the heat and drain; rinse well under cold running water. Drain well again and set aside.

Remove 2 tablespoons of duck fat from the baking dish and heat in a large skillet over medium heat. Add the apple slices and brown them on both sides. Remove the apples from the skillet and place them with the duck to keep warm.

Add the remaining vinegar to the skillet and cook over high heat for 1 minute. Add the cabbage, honey, thyme, black sesame seeds and the sesame oil. Mix well and cook for 2 minutes.

Cut the duck into 4 serving pieces and place them on a serving platter. Surround the duck with the cabbage; surround the cabbage with the apples and serve.

❦ Braised Duck with ❦ Fresh Mint

Serves 4

*I*n this recipe, remove the duck skin. This is very easy to do. With a sharp knife, make an incision along the backbone and cut the skin away from the meat. Remove as much duck fat as possible from the skin and set it aside to be used with the mint. You could ask the butcher to skin the duck for you, but be sure to tell him you want the skin and fat. Serve this dish with mashed potatoes.

1 bunch fresh mint, tough
    stems removed
1 large onion, quartered
salt
freshly ground black pepper
3 tablespoons vegetable oil

1 duck, skinned and cut into
    8 serving pieces
2 tablespoons all-purpose
    flour
2 cups dry white wine

Set aside 2 mint sprigs. Place the remaining mint sprigs, onion and salt and black pepper to taste in a food processor and process until finely chopped. Set aside.

In a large saucepan, heat the oil over high heat. Add the duck pieces and brown them on all sides. Remove the duck pieces to a platter.

Add the chopped mint mixture to the saucepan and sauté over medium heat for about 5 minutes. Sprinkle with the flour, mix well and add the white wine, stirring constantly. Add additional salt and black pepper to taste. Return the duck pieces, lower the heat, cover the saucepan and simmer for 45 minutes, or until the duck is easily pierced with a fork.

Chop the remaining mint leaves.

Place the duck pieces on a serving platter. Pour the sauce over them. Sprinkle with the chopped mint and serve.

Vegetables
and
Side Dishes

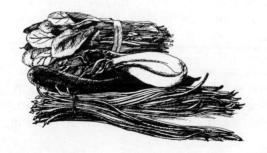

Vegetables

🍏 Stuffed Baby Zucchini 🍏

Serves 8

16 baby zucchini
salt
1 bunch scallions, trimmed
2 eggs
3 tablespoons chopped fresh
  basil or 1 tablespoon
  dried basil

2 tablespoons chopped
  chives
4 tablespoons grated
  Parmesan cheese
½ pound ricotta or farmer
  cheese
freshly ground black pepper
2 tablespoons olive oil

Cut the zucchini in half lengthwise. With a small spoon, scoop out and reserve the inside flesh, leaving shells about ¼ inch thick. Lightly sprinkle the zucchini shells with salt and set them aside.

Place the scallions in a food processor with the reserved zucchini flesh; process until finely chopped.

In a large mixing bowl, beat the eggs with a whisk until lightly frothy. Add the scallion-and-zucchini mixture and the basil, chives, Parmesan cheese and ricotta or farmer cheese. Add black pepper to taste and mix well with a fork.

Fill the zucchini shells with the cheese mixture. Arrange the zucchini on a platter. Brush the tops of the zucchini with the olive oil.

This dish can also be served hot. Arrange the stuffed zucchini in a single layer on a lightly-greased baking dish. Bake in the center of a 400°F oven for 20 minutes, until the cheese melts and they are lightly browned on top.

200

❦ Endives with Beets ❦

Serves 6 to 8

*J*ohn Githens is not only an unusual linguist (he writes and speaks at least six languages) but also a very inventive cook. One night at John's home, a group of us were talking about how cooks use the colors of their ingredients the way a painter uses his palette. When one of us disagreed, John left the room, went into the kitchen and came back a few minutes later with this vivid composition of endives and beets. He had won his point: Cooks are artists, with food as their palette!

4 fresh beets or 8 ounces canned beets	freshly ground black pepper
1 pound farmer cheese	1 tablespoon olive oil
salt	4 endives
	1 bunch curly parsley

If using fresh beets, trim them and scrub them well. Place them in a medium saucepan, add enough water to cover and bring to a boil. Reduce the heat to medium and cook until the beets are tender, about 45 minutes. Drain the beets; when cool, peel and quarter them. Set aside 1 beet.

Place the 3 other beets in a food processor with half the farmer cheese. Process until the ingredients are puréed. Pour into a bowl and add the remaining cheese, salt and black pepper to taste and the oil. Mix well.

Wipe the endives and separate all the leaves. Fill the large end of each endive leaf with a teaspoonful of the beet-and-cheese mixture. Arrange the stuffed leaves on a platter (if you have a black platter, the contrast of colors is magnificent), leaving a space in the center.

Julienne the remaining beet. Trim the parsley and place the sprigs in the center of the platter. Sprinkle the julienned beets over the filled endive leaves and serve.

❧ Potato Galettes ❧

Serves 6

*E*verybody's mother or grandmother has a recipe for potato pancakes, but my mother-in-law's potato pancakes were truly unique. The difference was that she added celery root purée to the grated potatoes, resulting in something more like a French galette than a pancake. Her secret, she used to say, was to soak the peeled potatoes in ice water and dry them well before grating, and to season the purée well.

These potato pancakes can be deep-fried or baked. Serve them with Crème Fraîche (see page 231) mixed with chopped tarragon or dill for a dairy lunch, or with roast chicken or beef for dinner.

1 large celery root, peeled and quartered
1 small onion, grated
1 teaspoon dried tarragon
salt
freshly ground black pepper
3 large baking potatoes
2 eggs

¼ teaspoon baking powder
about ½ cup all-purpose flour
2 cups very fine plain breadcrumbs
vegetable oil for frying or margarine for baking

Place the celery root in a medium saucepan. Cover with cold water, bring to a boil, reduce the heat to medium and cook for 20 minutes or until the celery root is easily pierced with a fork.

Drain the celery root over a saucepan or bowl (reserve the liquid for making vegetable stock). Cut the celery root into small pieces and mash them in a bowl. Add the onion, tarragon and salt and black pepper to taste. Set aside.

Peel the potatoes and place them in a large bowl. Add enough ice water to cover and let stand for 30 minutes. Drain the potatoes and pat them dry with paper towels.

Using the julienne blade of a food processor, julienne the potatoes.

Beat the eggs and add them to the celery purée; add the baking powder and salt and black pepper to taste. Mix well.

Add the julienned potatoes to the purée and mix gently. Add enough of the flour to make a dough thick enough to roll.

On a floured board, roll out the dough to a ¼-inch thickness. With a large round cookie cutter or a teacup, cut out 12 to 15 circles. Dredge each circle with the breadcrumbs.

To fry the potato pancakes, heat ½ inch of vegetable oil in a deep skillet. When the oil is very hot, carefully drop in some of the potato circles and fry until they are golden brown all over, about 2 minutes, turning them once with a metal spatula. Drain on paper towels and keep warm in a low oven until all the pancakes are done.

To bake the potato pancakes, preheat the oven to 425°F. Grease a baking sheet with margarine. Place the potato circles on the baking sheet, leaving some space between them. Bake until golden brown, about 5 to 8 minutes.

❦ Potato Latkes ❦

Serves 4

*E*veryone *I spoke with while researching this book gave me a recipe for potato latkes. I tried them all, changed them, added other ingredients and came up with this recipe. It's not quite traditional, but it's delicious.*

6 medium potatoes, peeled
2 onions
1 teaspoon salt
freshly ground black pepper
3 tablespoons matzo meal
½ teaspoon baking powder
1 egg

vegetable oil for frying
1 tablespoon black sesame
  seeds
1 pint sour cream
2 scallions, finely chopped
parsley sprigs, for garnish
1 pint applesauce (optional)

Grate the potatoes, using the fine side of a grater or the fine julienne blade of a food processor. Place the potatoes in a large mixing bowl and rinse thoroughly with cold water. Drain the potatoes in a colander, shaking the colander several times to remove as much water as possible. Put the potatoes back into the mixing bowl.

Grate the onions finely and add them to the potatoes. Add the salt, black pepper to taste, the matzo meal, baking powder and egg. Mix well.

In a large skillet, heat 2 tablespoons of the oil over medium heat. Drop in tablespoons of the potato mixture. Sprinkle some black sesame seeds on top of each latke. Cook until the latkes are browned on the bottom, about 2 to 3 minutes. With a spatula, turn the latkes over and cook until browned on the other side. Drain on paper towels, then transfer to an ovenproof dish. Keep the latkes warm in a low oven. Add more oil to the skillet as needed and continue to make latkes until all the potato mixture is used.

In a bowl, mix the sour cream with the scallions.

Place the latkes on a serving platter and garnish with parsley sprigs. Serve with the sour cream mixture or applesauce.

🥜 Lentils with Sorrel 🥜

Serves 6

1 pound brown lentils
¼ pound red lentils
6 cups cold water
salt
freshly ground black pepper
1 pound fresh sorrel
¼ cup water

1 tablespoon sugar
2 tablespoons duck or
   chicken fat
4 garlic cloves, thinly sliced
2 tablespoons chopped
   parsley

Put the brown and red lentils in a large saucepan with the cold water. Bring the water to a boil over high heat; reduce the heat to a simmer. Add salt and black pepper to taste. Simmer until the lentils are tender but not mushy, about 40 minutes. Drain well and set the lentils aside.

Rinse the sorrel well and trim away any tough stems and discolored leaves. Place the sorrel in the same saucepan used for the lentils and add ¼ cup water and the sugar. Bring to a boil, stir well and remove from the heat. Add the lentils to the sorrel and mix well.

Melt the duck fat in a small skillet over medium heat. Add the garlic and sauté until it is golden. Add the duck fat and garlic to the lentil mixture. Mix well.

Just before serving, gently warm the mixture over low heat. Spoon it into a serving dish and sprinkle with the chopped parsley.

Bavarois of Red
🍃 Peppers with 🍃
Parsley Sauce

Serves 4

2 large sweet red peppers
1 sprig fresh rosemary or
    ½ teaspoon dried
    rosemary
2 garlic cloves, peeled
¼ teaspoon cayenne pepper
salt
freshly ground black pepper
2 silken bean curd cakes

2 envelopes unflavored
    gelatine
3 tablespoons cold water
¾ cups Chicken Stock (see
    page 49)
1 tablespoon vegetable oil
2 cups Parsley Sauce (see
    page 234)
4 small parsley sprigs, for
    garnish

In a bamboo or metal steamer, steam the red peppers with
the rosemary sprig for 3 minutes. Immediately transfer them
to a large bowl of cold water.

Drain the peppers. Peel them and then cut them in two;
remove the seeds and stems and cut each half in several
pieces.

Place the red pepper pieces, rosemary sprig, garlic,
cayenne pepper, salt and black pepper to taste and the bean
curd in a food processor. Process until the ingredients are
puréed. Strain the mixture through a fine sieve into a large
mixing bowl. Set aside.

In a small bowl, dissolve the gelatine in the cold water. In
a small saucepan, bring the Chicken Stock to a boil. Add the
gelatine, lower the heat and simmer, stirring constantly, until
the gelatine has dissolved completely.

Add the gelatine mixture to the red pepper purée. Mix
well and add additional salt and pepper to taste.

Oil four 4-ounce molds with the vegetable oil. Fill the molds with the red pepper mixture and refrigerate for 4 hours or overnight.

To serve, pour some of the Parsley Sauce onto each of 4 individual serving plates. Unmold a bavarois on top of the sauce on each plate. Garnish the tops with parsley sprigs.

Steamed Swiss Chard with Thyme

Serves 6

S wiss chard is a wonderful vegetable that is often ignored. There are two kinds of Swiss chard: one with white stems, which is the most widely available variety; and one with red stems, which I find not only more beautiful but also sweeter in taste. Either kind can be used in this recipe.

3 pounds Swiss chard
2 tablespoons chopped fresh
   thyme or 1 teaspoon
   dried thyme

1½ tablespoons lemon juice
2 tablespoons olive oil
salt
freshly ground black pepper

Rinse the Swiss chard and pat it dry. With a sharp knife, remove the tough stalks and discard them (or reserve them for a vegetable soup). Steam the chard in a bamboo or metal steamer for 2 minutes. Remove to a serving platter and keep warm.

Mix the lemon thyme, lemon juice and olive oil together in a bowl. Add salt and black pepper to taste. Pour the sauce over the Swiss chard and serve.

207

Spaghetti Squash with ❧ Mushroom Sauce and ❧ Smoked Salmon

Serves 6

1 large spaghetti squash,
about 2 pounds
4 tablespoons unsalted
butter
2 garlic cloves, chopped
3 tablespoons chopped
parsley
1 pound white mushrooms,
coarsely chopped

½ cup Vegetable Stock (see
page 44)
½ cup dry white wine
salt
freshly ground black pepper
½ pound sliced smoked
salmon, coarsely
chopped
parsley sprigs, for garnish

Preheat the oven to 450°F.

Place the spaghetti squash on a baking sheet and bake for 35 minutes or until it can easily be pierced with a fork. Remove the squash from the oven, cut it in half lengthwise and use a fork to remove the flesh, which resembles strands of spaghetti. Place the strands in a serving bowl and keep warm.

In a large skillet, melt the butter over medium heat. Add the garlic and parsley; cook for 2 to 3 minutes. Add the mushrooms and sauté for 4 minutes. Add the Vegetable Stock, wine and salt and black pepper to taste; cook for another 5 minutes over medium heat. Remove from the heat and set aside.

Add the mushroom sauce and the smoked salmon to the spaghetti squash. Toss well, garnish with parsley sprigs and serve.

❦ Braised Salsify ❦

Serves 6

S *alsify is a long, thin black root shaped like an overextended carrot. For years, salsify was eaten in the United States only by the French and Italians. Today it can be found in markets all over the country. Before cooking, salsify should be peeled or scraped just like a carrot; but the peeled roots should then be placed immediately in a bowl of water with 2 teaspoons of vinegar, or they will turn brown.*

2 pounds salsify
2 tablespoons wine vinegar
2 quarts water
1 teaspoon salt
2 tablespoons olive oil
2 garlic cloves, sliced
1 tablespoon all-purpose
   flour

⅛ teaspoon cinnamon
1 cup Chicken Stock (see
   page 49)
freshly ground black pepper
2 tablespoons chopped
   parsley

Peel the salsify, rinse thoroughly and cut the roots into 2-inch pieces. Place the pieces in a large bowl, add enough cold water to cover and add the vinegar.

In a saucepan, bring the 2 quarts water and the salt to a boil. Drain the salsify pieces and add them to the boiling water. Bring the water back to the boiling point, reduce the heat to medium, cover and cook the salsify for 1 hour, or until it is tender when pierced with a fork. Drain and set aside.

In a large skillet, heat the oil over medium heat. Add the garlic and sauté until it is light brown. Add the salsify and sauté for 2 to 3 minutes. Sprinkle the pieces with the flour and mix well; sprinkle with the cinnamon and mix well again. Add the Chicken Stock and black pepper, reduce the heat and simmer for 15 minutes. Serve sprinkled with the chopped parsley.

209

Cowpeas with Polish Mushrooms

Serves 8

B *eans. The word evokes for me the cold winter days of my childhood, when after playing in the snow we would run home and have a hot bowl of lentils. My grandmother was an extraordinary magician with any kind of dried bean or legume. She used lentils, green peas, black beans and cowpeas in salads and soups, and as vegetables served with fish, chicken or lamb. In most supermarkets today, there are many different kinds of dried beans. Cowpeas come from Colombia. They are rich in protein, but above all they are very tasty and make a superb complement to roast lamb or chicken. If you cannot find cowpeas, black-eyed peas may be substituted.*

1 pound dried cowpeas or
    black-eyed peas
3 tablespoons olive oil
2 garlic cloves, sliced
¼ cup light soy sauce or
    low-sodium soy sauce
2 tablespoons drained
    capers

2 bay leaves
½ ounce dried Polish
    mushrooms, soaked
    1 hour in cold water to
    cover
salt
freshly ground black pepper

To make in advance, place the cowpeas in a large bowl; cover them with cold water and soak overnight. Drain well.

To cook the same day, place the cowpeas in a saucepan and cover them with boiling water. Let stand for 2 hours, then drain and proceed.

In a large saucepan, heat the oil over medium-high heat. Add the garlic and sauté until golden brown. Add the cowpeas and mix well. Add enough cold water to cover the beans; then add 1 cup of water more. Add the soy sauce, capers, bay leaves and Polish mushrooms. Bring the water to a boil, lower the heat, cover and simmer for 1½ hours, or until the beans are tender (check from time to time and add more water if necessary). Add salt and black pepper to taste and serve.

The cowpeas can also be cooled and then frozen, or refrigerated for several days.

꒒ Steamed Spinach ꒒ with Garlic

Serves 6

This spinach should be cooked at the last minute when preparing it as a side dish for a meat or fish course. If serving the spinach with Chicken-Stuffed Steamed Cabbage (see page 156), use only 1 tablespoon olive oil.

4 pounds spinach, washed and trimmed
2 tablespoons olive oil

2 garlic cloves, finely chopped
salt
freshly ground black pepper

Steam the spinach in a bamboo or metal steamer for 3 minutes. Remove from the heat immediately.

In a small saucepan, heat the oil over medium heat; add the garlic and sauté until it is golden brown.

Place the spinach in a large serving bowl. Sprinkle it with salt and black pepper to taste and pour the oil and garlic over it. Toss well and serve.

❦ Garlic Purée ❦

Serves 6

*T*his recipe is superb, but it requires patience to peel a pound of garlic. The purée will keep for several days if refrigerated and can be frozen for future use. Serve it with chicken or veal dishes.

1 pound garlic cloves, peeled
4 tablespoons goose or
   chicken fat
2 silken bean curd cakes

salt
freshly ground black pepper
3 parsley sprigs, for garnish

Place the garlic cloves in a saucepan, add enough water to cover and bring to a boil. Drain the garlic, then return it to the saucepan with the goose fat. Cook over high heat for 2 minutes, lower the heat and simmer, covered, for 15 minutes or until the garlic is very soft. Drain well.

    Place the garlic, bean curd and salt and black pepper to taste in a food processor. Process until the ingredients are puréed. Pour into a bowl. Serve garnished with the parsley sprigs.

❧ James's Fried ❧ Onion Rings

Serves 4

I *had never eaten fried onion rings until I came to America. One night my husband, James, decided that he would take over the kitchen and make me fried onions. The end results of this historical event were: (1) I ate superb fried onions; (2) It took me 3 hours to clean the kitchen; (3) I decided that I had to learn how to make them if I wanted to save my marriage!*

The secret of great, grease-free fried onion rings, my husband says, is a brown paper bag.

4 large Spanish onions (about 2 pounds), thinly sliced and separated into rings
3 cups milk
4 cups all-purpose flour

2 garlic cloves, grated
salt
freshly ground black pepper
vegetable oil for deep frying
parsley sprigs, for garnish

In a large mixing bowl, place the onion rings and cover them with the milk. Let them stand in the milk for ½ hour to remove any bitterness from the onions.

Put the flour, garlic, salt and pepper in a brown paper bag and shake well.

Drain the onion rings and put them into the paper bag. Close with a metal tie or twist the top. Shake the bag well until all the onion rings are coated with flour.

Heat the oil in a deep-fryer or deep heavy skillet until it reaches 365°F on a deep-frying thermometer. Then fry some of the onion rings until golden brown. Remove with a wire skimmer and drain on paper towels; place on a serving platter and keep warm in a 200°F oven until all the onion rings are done.

Serve garnished with parsley.

213

❦ Pumpkin Flan ❦

Serves 6

*T*his recipe makes a beautiful accompaniment to a
baked whole fish. Place the fish on a serving platter and
surround it with the pumpkin flans and thin slices of
orange.

4 eggs
1 1-pound can pumpkin purée
1 cup heavy cream
1 teaspoon brandy
⅛ teaspoon nutmeg
grated zest of 2 oranges

salt
freshly ground black pepper
butter
1 orange, unpeeled and
    thinly sliced, for garnish

Preheat the oven to 425°F.

In a large bowl, beat the eggs; add the pumpkin purée,
cream, brandy, nutmeg, orange zest and salt and black
pepper to taste. Mix well with a wire whisk.

Generously butter 6 individual 3-ounce molds. Fill the
molds with the pumpkin mixture.

Place the molds in a baking pan; fill the pan halfway with
water and bake for 25 minutes or until a thin skewer inserted
into the center of a flan comes out clean.

Unmold the flans onto a flat plate and garnish with
orange slices. Serve them carefully with a spatula.

Grains

___

❧ Farfel Pan Stuffing ❧

Serves 8

*W*hen cooked in broth and seasoned, farfel becomes a *wonderful companion to poultry, especially roast duck or broiled quails. Whenever I cook a turkey or a goose, I freeze the leftover gravy to use later in dishes such as this.*

2 tablespoons goose fat or
    chicken fat
1 onion, thinly sliced
1 cup farfel
3 cups Chicken Stock (see
    page 49)
¼ teaspoon ground cumin
salt

freshly ground black pepper
½ cup leftover gravy or
    2 tablespoons light soy
    sauce
zest of 1 lemon or lime,
    julienned
2 tablespoons chopped
    parsley

In a large, deep skillet, melt the fat over medium heat. Add the onion and sauté until it is transparent but not brown. Add the farfel and sauté until it is golden brown. Add the Chicken Stock, cumin, and salt and black pepper to taste and mix well. Reduce the heat and simmer, covered, until all the liquid has been absorbed.

When the farfel is tender but still firm, add the gravy or soy sauce, citrus zest and parsley. Mix well and cook, uncovered, for another 4 to 5 minutes.

215

৶ Rice Turban with ৶ Green Peas

Serves 6

*U*se long-grain rice for this dish. You will need a ceramic ring-shaped savarin mold of about 4 to 5 cups' capacity. For a main course, try filling the center of the unmolded turban with a Blanquette de Veau (see page 143).

2 tablespoons vegetable oil
2 cups long-grain rice
½ tablespoon fennel seeds
salt
freshly ground black pepper
3 cups boiling water
½ pound frozen tiny peas

2 cups water
1 teaspoon salt
½ pound frozen tiny peas
1 tablespoon black sesame
   seeds
2 small parsley sprigs, for
   garnish

In a heavy saucepan, heat 1½ tablespoons of the oil over medium heat. When the oil is hot, add the rice and sauté for 2 minutes, stirring constantly with a wooden spoon. Add the fennel seeds and salt and black pepper to taste; mix well. Add the boiling water, bring back to a boil, cover, lower the heat and cook for 20 minutes, or until all the water has been absorbed and the rice is tender.

In a small saucepan, bring 2 cups of water with 1 teaspoon salt to a boil. Add the frozen peas, bring to a boil again and turn off the heat. Let the peas stand in the water for 2 to 3 minutes, then drain well.

Add the peas and sesame seeds to the cooked rice and mix well. (Be careful not to squash the peas.)

Lightly oil the savarin mold with the remaining vegetable oil. Fill the mold with the rice-and-pea mixture, pressing it down with the back of a wooden spoon.

Unmold the turban of rice onto a round platter. Garnish the center with parsley sprigs, their stems pointing downward. If the center is to be filled, add the filling just before serving. Serve immediately.

❦ Toasted Farfel ❦

Serves 4

S erve this as a side dish with roast chicken.

2 tablespoons goose or
   chicken fat
1 onion, thinly sliced
1 cup farfel

3 cups Chicken Stock (see
   page 49)
salt
freshly ground black pepper

In a large, deep skillet over medium heat, melt the fat. Add the onion and sauté until it is transparent but not brown. Add the farfel and sauté until it is golden brown. Add the Chicken Stock and salt and black pepper to taste. Mix well. Reduce the heat and simmer, covered, until all the liquid has been absorbed.

Preheat the oven to 375°F.

Remove the cover and continue to cook, stirring constantly, until the farfel is dry. Remove from the heat and spread the farfel in a baking dish.

Bake until the farfel is golden brown, about 10 minutes.

❧ Kasha with Eggplant ❧

Serves 6

My daughter Marianne developed this wonderful recipe, which combines the earthy, nutty flavor of kasha with the silken qualities of eggplant. The ginger gives it just the bite and freshness to make it unusual.

2 cups whole-grain kasha
2 eggs, beaten
1 teaspoon salt
¾ teaspoon freshly ground black pepper
4 cups Chicken Stock (see page 49)

6 tiny purple eggplants, about 2 pounds total
2 tablespoons olive oil
1 large garlic clove, chopped
1 teaspoon grated fresh ginger or ½ teaspoon dried ground ginger
parsley sprigs, for garnish

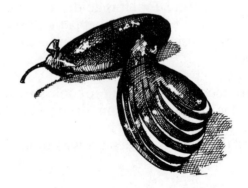

Place the kasha in a skillet and add the beaten eggs. Mix well.
Dry the kasha over medium heat, stirring constantly with a
wooden spoon until all the grains are separate, 2 to 3 minutes.
Add salt and black pepper to taste and 2 cups of the Chicken
Stock. Bring to a boil, lower the heat and simmer, covered,
until all the liquid is absorbed. (If the kasha is not totally
cooked at this point add ½ cup Chicken Stock and simmer
until it is absorbed.) Set the kasha aside and keep it warm in
a low oven.

While the kasha is cooking, trim the ends from the
eggplants. Slice the eggplants in half lengthwise without
cutting all the way to the end (see illustration).

Heat the olive oil in a medium skillet over medium heat.
Add the garlic and sauté for 1 minute; add the eggplants and
sauté for 2 minutes. Add the ginger and the remaining 1½
cups of the Chicken Stock. Lower the heat, correct the
seasoning and simmer for 5 minutes, or until the eggplants
are soft when pierced with a fork.

To serve, place the kasha in a round serving bowl. Make
a well in the center. Place the eggplants in the center, the
wide ends of the eggplants facing out. Pour the sauce from
the skillet over the kasha. Garnish with parsley sprigs and
serve.

Toasted Couscous with Eggplant

Serves 4

C *ouscous, a light, fine-grained semolina pasta, is the national dish of several North African countries. Generally couscous is quite small, but a large-grained variety of toasted couscous is made in Israel and is available in kosher supermarkets. It is excellent with onions and eggplant. Serve it with steak, fish or chicken.*

2 quarts water
salt
8 ounces toasted large-grain
  couscous
2 small eggplants, totaling
  about ½ pound
3 tablespoons olive oil

1 medium onion, thinly
  sliced
freshly ground black pepper
1 sprig fresh marjoram
¼ teaspoon ground cumin
6 black Greek olives, pitted
  and chopped

In a large saucepan, salt the water to taste and bring to a boil. Add the couscous, stir well, lower the heat and simmer, uncovered, for 8 minutes or until the couscous is tender but firm. Drain immediately in a fine-mesh colander and rinse well with cold water to keep the couscous from sticking together.

Trim the eggplant stems and cut the eggplants into ¼-inch slices.

In a medium saucepan, heat the oil over high heat. Add the sliced onion and eggplant, reduce the heat to medium and cook for 5 minutes, stirring constantly, until the onions are transparent and the eggplant soft. Sprinkle with salt and black pepper to taste; add the fresh marjoram and the cumin.

Add the couscous and the olives. Mix well and cook for 5 minutes over medium heat. Serve immediately.

Pastas

❦ Thomas's Spaghetti ❦

Serves 4

My son Thomas spent six months in Siena, Italy, living with an Italian family. In each letter home, he would describe a new pasta dish and enclose the recipe. The one I liked the best was spaghetti with oil, garlic and anchovies. Whenever Thomas does the cooking, I insist that he make that recipe.

3 quarts water
½ tablespoon salt
1 cup olive oil
4 large garlic cloves, sliced
¼ teaspoon freshly ground
   black pepper
1 pound thin spaghetti

4 anchovy fillets, drained,
   1 teaspoon of their oil
   reserved
2 tablespoons drained
   capers
3 tablespoons chopped
   parsley

In a large pot, bring the water and ½ tablespoon salt to a boil.

While waiting for the water to boil, pour the olive oil into a medium saucepan over medium heat. Add the garlic and black pepper and sauté until the garlic is golden brown. Set aside and keep warm.

Cook the spaghetti in the boiling water until it is *al dente*.

While the spaghetti cooks, coarsely chop the anchovies. Place them in a bowl; add the anchovy oil, capers and parsley and mix well.

Drain the spaghetti and place it in a deep bowl. Pour the hot oil with the garlic and the anchovy mixture over the spaghetti. Toss well.

221

Fresh Pasta with
🍒 Tomato Mushroom 🍒
Sauce

Serves 4

*I*f *fresh pasta is not available, use dried tagliatelli or
broad egg noodles.*

1 pound mushrooms	2 tablespoons olive oil
2 cups packed fresh basil	½ tablespoon oregano
leaves	4 quarts water
1 bunch parsley	1 teaspoon salt
2 garlic cloves	1 teaspoon vegetable oil
salt	1 pound fresh pasta,
freshly ground black pepper	preferably tagliatelli
1 1-pound can whole	2 ounces grated Parmesan
tomatoes	cheese

Wash, trim and drain the mushrooms. Set aside 10
mushrooms.

Place the remaining mushrooms, the basil, parsley and
garlic in a food processor. Process until the ingredients are
puréed. (If your food processor has a small bowl, purée the
ingredients in batches.)

Pour the mushroom mixture into a large skillet. Add salt
and black pepper to taste, mix well and set aside.

Slice the reserved mushrooms. Drain the liquid from the
tomatoes, being careful not to break them. Add the sliced
mushrooms, tomatoes, olive oil and oregano to the skillet.
Gently stir the mixture over medium heat until the mushrooms
are cooked, about 4 minutes. Remove from the heat and
keep warm.

Bring the water to a boil in a large saucepan. Add the 1 teaspoon salt and the vegetable oil. Add the pasta, bring back to a boil and cook until it is *al dente*, about 5 minutes. Drain well.

Place the pasta in a large round serving bowl. Pour the mushroom sauce over it and serve with the grated Parmesan cheese.

❦ Fresh Tagliatelli ❦
with Walnuts

Serves 6

G ood fresh pasta is easy to make if you have a pasta machine. And today it is even easier to buy fresh flat tagliatelli pasta in speciality stores and supermarkets. You could also use dry egg noodles for this recipe.

2 quarts water
1 tablespoon vegetable oil
1 teaspoon salt
6 tablespoons unsalted
    butter
¼ pound shelled walnuts,
    finely chopped

2 teaspoons sugar
⅛ teaspoon cinnamon
salt
freshly ground black pepper
1 pound fresh pasta,
    preferably tagliatelli

In a large saucepan, bring the water, oil and salt to a boil.

While waiting for the water to boil, melt the butter in a small saucepan over medium heat; add the walnuts, sugar and cinnamon and salt and black pepper to taste. Mix well and cook for 3 minutes. Remove from the heat and keep warm.

Cook the pasta in the boiling water until it is *al dente*, about 4 minutes. Drain well and place in a large bowl. Add the walnut-and-butter mixture, toss gently and serve.

223

❧ Kate Goldstein's ❧ Noodle Pudding

Serves 6

*N*oodle pudding, like all puddings, is not as good cold. If you are baking the pudding ahead of time, keep it warm in a very low oven, covered with aluminum foil, so that it doesn't get dry.

2 quarts water
1 teaspoon vegetable oil
1 pound medium egg
   noodles
6 eggs
3 cups milk
1 pint sour cream
1 pint cottage cheese
½ cup currants

½ cup dried apricots, cut in
   small pieces
6 tablespoons sugar
1½ teaspoons vanilla
   extract
¼ pound unsalted butter
¼ cup confectioner's sugar
   mixed with ½ teaspoon
   cinnamon

Preheat the oven to 350°F.

In a large saucepan, bring the water to a boil. Add the vegetable oil. When the water returns to the boil, add the egg noodles. Cook until tender but still firm, about 3 minutes. Drain the noodles and place them in a large bowl.

In another bowl, beat the eggs with a wire whisk. Add them to the noodles and mix well. In the same bowl used for the eggs, mix together the milk, sour cream, cottage cheese, currants, apricots, sugar and vanilla; stir well after adding each ingredient. Pour the mixture into the noodles and mix well.

In a small saucepan, melt the butter but do not let it brown. Pour the butter into a 9-by-9-by-2-inch baking pan. Pour the noodle mixture into the baking pan and bake for about 1 hour and 10 minutes, until firm and lightly browned. Remove from the oven, sprinkle the top with cinnamon and sugar and serve at room temperature.

☙ Rice Noodles ❧

Serves 4

*R*ice noodles come in packages that are sometimes labeled "saifun noodles". Deep-fried straight from the package, they puff up and turn white. (Cooked in water, they can be added to soups or salads.)

5-ounce package rice or saifun noodles

2 cups vegetable oil for deep frying
1 Boston lettuce

Separate the noodles into 3 to 4 batches. In a deep-fryer or a deep heavy skillet, heat the oil until it reaches 365°F on a deep-frying thermometer. Fry the noodles one batch at a time; they will immediately puff up into snowy strands. With a wire skimmer, remove at once before they brown; drain on paper towels.

Line a serving dish with Boston lettuce leaves and place the fried noodles on top.

Serve with chicken or fish, or add to salad.

Baked Macaroni ❧ with Mushroom ❧ Cream Sauce

Serves 4

1 pound elbow macaroni or
small ziti
6 egg yolks, lightly beaten
2 ounces grated Swiss cheese
2 ounces grated Parmesan
cheese

¼ pound mushrooms, sliced
⅛ teaspoon nutmeg
salt
freshly ground black pepper
6 egg whites

Mushroom Cream Sauce:
2 tablespoons unsalted
butter, plus additional
butter for mold
¼ pound mushrooms,
coarsely chopped
1 ounce dried Polish
mushrooms, soaked for
1 hour in 1 cup of water

salt
freshly ground black pepper
1 cup heavy cream
1 tablespoon chopped
parsley

Cook the macaroni in a large pot of boiling salted water until it is *al dente*. Drain well and place in a large bowl. Add the egg yolks, Swiss cheese, Parmesan cheese, mushrooms, nutmeg and salt and black pepper to taste. Mix well. Taste the mixture: it should be quite peppery.

In another bowl, beat the egg whites until they hold a peak. Gently fold the egg whites into the macaroni mixture.

Preheat the oven to 350°F. Butter a 2½-quart mold.

Pour the macaroni mixture into the mold. Place the mold in a baking pan half-filled with water. Cover the mold with aluminum foil. Bake for 45 minutes or until a cake tester inserted into the center comes out clean.

Meanwhile, make the sauce. In a saucepan, melt the butter over medium-to-high heat. When the butter foams, add the chopped mushrooms and the dried mushrooms with their soaking liquid. Reduce the heat to medium and cook for 5 minutes. Add salt and black pepper to taste, mix well and cook for another 5 minutes. Set aside.

Remove the mold from the oven and unmold it onto a round platter.

Add the cream to the sauce. Cook over low heat just until the sauce is hot; do not let it boil. Pour the sauce over the macaroni, sprinkle with the parsley and serve.

🍒 Seme di Melone with 🍒 Mushroom Sauce

Serves 6

S eme di melone are very tiny noodles shaped like melon seeds. They can be found in any well-stocked Italian grocery store; if unavailable, they can be replaced by orzo, small rice-shaped pasta.

½ cup dried shiitake
   mushrooms
2 ounces dried Polish
   mushrooms
1 pound white mushrooms
2 tablespoons vegetable oil
2 garlic cloves, sliced
3 cups Vegetable Stock

1 tablespoon dark soy sauce
salt
freshly ground black pepper
4 quarts water
1 16-ounce box seme di
   melone or orzo
2 ounces grated Parmesan
   cheese

In a bowl, soak the shiitake and Polish mushrooms in enough water to cover for 30 minutes. Cut and discard the stems from the mushrooms and slice the caps; reserve the soaking liquid.

Remove the stems from the white mushrooms and reserve them for a soup. Slice the caps.

In a deep skillet, heat the oil over high heat. Add the garlic and sauté until it is light golden brown. Add all the mushrooms and sauté for 2 to 3 minutes, stirring with a wooden spoon. Add the Vegetable Stock, soy sauce and salt and black pepper to taste. Bring to a boil, reduce the heat and simmer, uncovered, for 15 minutes.

In a large saucepan, bring the 2 quarts of water to a boil. Add the seme di melone and cook for 5 minutes or until they are *al dente*. Drain well through a very fine strainer. Pour the pasta into a large serving bowl. Pour the mushroom sauce over them and serve with the Parmesan cheese.

228

Sauces

❦ Anchovy Vinaigrette ❦

Makes ½ cup

2 anchovy fillets, drained,
   1 tablespoon anchovy oil
   reserved

2 tablespoons wine vinegar
4 tablespoons olive oil
freshly ground black pepper

With a fork, mash the anchovies with their oil. Add the vinegar and mix well. Stir in the olive oil and the pepper and serve.

❦ Classic Vinaigrette ❦

Makes ¼ cup

2 tablespoons extra-virgin
   olive oil
1 tablespoon wine vinegar

1 teaspoon strong Dijon
   mustard
salt
freshly ground black pepper

In a small bowl, combine all the ingredients. Whisk until well blended.

❦ Crème Fraîche ❦

Makes 2 cups

1 cup heavy cream
1 cup sour cream

Combine the heavy cream and the sour cream in a small bowl. Whisk to blend well.

Cover the bowl loosely with aluminum foil and let stand in a warm place overnight or until thick. This could take 12 or more hours.

Cover the bowl tightly and refrigerate for at least 12 hours before serving.

❦ Tahini Sauce ❦

Makes 2 cups

1 cup tahini
about ½ cup water
6 tablespoons lemon juice
salt

freshly ground black pepper
¼ teaspoon cumin
1 garlic clove, finely
    chopped

Place the tahini in a bowl; add the water and stir until the mixture has the consistency of thick cream, adding a little more water, if necessary, to achieve the right consistency.

Add the lemon juice, cumin, garlic and salt and black pepper to taste. Mix well and adjust the seasoning. Store in a covered glass jar and refrigerate until ready to use.

❦ Yakitori Sauce ❦

Makes 1½ cups

*Y*akitori Sauce is used by Japanese cooks whenever they broil meats, fish or vegetables. It is made with sake, the Japanese rice wine, mirin, which is heavily sweetened rice wine, somewhat like a cross between a golden syrup and dark soy sauce. When ingredients are marinated or brushed with this mixture, they broil to a rich golden brown glaze and develop a slight caramel taste.

8 tablespoons sake
8 tablespoons mirin (sweet
   rice wine)

8 tablespoons dark soy
   sauce
1 tablespoon sugar

In a medium saucepan, bring all the ingredients to a boil; reduce the heat and simmer until all the sugar has dissolved. Cool to room temperature and pour into a glass jar. Refrigerate until ready to use.

❦ Teriyaki Sauce ❦

Makes 3 cups

*T*eriyaki is the Japanese word applied to meats, fish or vegetables that have been marinated in a sweet mixture of mirin and soy sauce, which gives the food a rich, lustrous surface when cooked.

1 cup mirin (sweet rice wine)
1 cup dark soy sauce

1 cup Chicken Stock (see
   page 49)

In a medium saucepan over medium heat, heat the mirin until hot but not yet boiling. Remove the saucepan from the heat and carefully ignite the mirin with a match to burn off the alcohol. Gently shake the saucepan until the flames die.

Add the soy sauce and the Chicken Stock. Bring to a boil over medium heat and turn off the heat. Allow the sauce to cool to room temperature. Pour into a glass jar and refrigerate until ready to use.

❦ Garlic Butter ❦

Makes 2 cups

*T*his aromatic butter freezes well. Defrost it overnight in the refrigerator and beat it with a whisk or a fork before serving.

For freezing, I often make little balls the size of a quarter and wrap them in individual pieces of plastic. When I poach fish steaks, I then place small pats of the butter on each steak, without having to defrost a large quantity.

4 garlic cloves
3 shallots
1 bunch curly parsley, stems
  removed
1 tablespoon almond
  powder

½ pound unsalted butter, at
  room temperature, cut
  into small pieces
salt
freshly ground black pepper

Place the garlic, shallots, parsley and almond powder in a food processor and process until finely chopped. Add the butter and process until well blended.

Remove the butter mixture to a bowl and add salt and black pepper to taste. Refrigerate until ready to serve.

Remove from the refrigerator at least 20 minutes before serving to let the butter soften to a spreadable consistency.

❦ Garlic Sauce ❦

Makes ¾ cup

5 tablespoons wine vinegar
5 tablespoons tomato juice
2 tablespoons olive oil
4 garlic cloves, quartered
2 teaspoons dried tarragon

2 teaspoons chopped fresh
   chives
salt
freshly ground black pepper

Place all the ingredients in a food processor and process until puréed. Pour into a bowl and refrigerate until ready to use.

❦ Parsley Sauce ❦

Makes 2 cups

2 cups Beef Stock (see
   page 46)
2 tablespoons cornstarch
3 tablespoons cold water
2 bunches parsley, tough
   stems removed
1 medium shallot

½ cup dry white wine
½ teaspoon lemon juice
salt
freshly ground black pepper
1 tablespoon chopped fresh
   parsley

In a small saucepan, bring the Beef Stock to a boil. Reduce the heat and simmer for 15 minutes.

In a small bowl, dissolve the cornstarch in the water.

Add the cornstarch to the stock and cook, stirring, until the liquid thickens. Set aside and keep warm.

Place the parsley, shallot, white wine and lemon juice in a food processor. Process until the solid ingredients are finely chopped.

Pour the parsley mixture into the Beef Stock. Simmer for 10 minutes more.

Strain the sauce through a fine sieve into a bowl. Add salt and black pepper to taste.

Serve in a sauceboat with the chopped parsley on top.

Sweet Red Pepper Sauce

Makes 2 cups

*T*his sauce can be refrigerated for several days in a tightly sealed glass jar.

2 large sweet red peppers, stemmed, seeded and cut into several pieces
1 cup Chicken Stock (see page 49) or Vegetable Stock (see page 44)

1 teaspoon sesame oil
salt
freshly ground black pepper
1 tablespoon chopped fresh chives

Place the sweet red peppers and chicken stock in a saucepan. Bring to a boil and cook, uncovered, over medium heat for 5 minutes.

Place the red peppers, stock, sesame oil, salt and black pepper in a food processor. Process until the red peppers are puréed.

Pour the purée into a bowl. Add additional salt and black pepper to taste and stir in the chopped chives.

235

❧ Fresh Uncooked ❧ Tomato Coulis

Makes 2 cups

*T*his recipe *must be made with fresh tomatoes. In the winter, when the tomatoes are not at their best, add 1 tablespoon of tomato paste to enhance the sauce's color. When serving this sauce with broiled fish, add some chopped black Greek olives. The sauce can be kept refrigerated for a few days in a tightly sealed jar.*

6 large beefsteak tomatoes,
   about 4 pounds
1 large garlic clove
2 tablespoons olive oil
1 tablespoon dried tarragon
1 tablespoon lime juice

1 tablespoon tomato paste
   (optional)
4 black Greek olives, pitted
   (optional)
salt
freshly ground black pepper

Cook the tomatoes in a large pot of boiling water for 2 to 3 minutes. Drain well and rinse under cold running water; drain well again. With a sharp knife, peel the tomatoes, then cut them in half and remove the seeds with a spoon. Squeeze the tomatoes with your fingers to remove any water.

Place the tomatoes and all the other ingredients in a food processor. Process until smoothly puréed. Pour the coulis into a bowl or jar and refrigerate until ready to use.

❦ Aïoli ❦

Makes 1½ cups

When I was first married, I served the rich garlic mayonnaise known as aïoli whenever I wanted to be original, which meant every other day. One day, when he once again found I was serving aïoli with the roast chicken, my husband placed a small roll of paper on my plate. It was a cartoon of me in a cloud of garlic, surrounded by little children running away.

I got the message, and aïoli became one of the dishes I made only once in a while. It is, however, excellent and essential with Potée (see page 125) and with Calf's-Foot Jelly (see page 38). Aïoli can keep refrigerated in a tightly sealed jar for one week.

2 slices white bread, soaked
   in water
6 large garlic cloves
1 cup olive oil

salt
freshly ground black pepper
3 tablespoons lemon juice

Squeeze all the water from the bread. Place the garlic and the bread in a food processor. Process until the ingredients are puréed. With the food processor still running, slowly add the olive oil in a thin steady stream, processing until the mixture is thick and creamy.

Remove the aïoli to a bowl and add salt and black pepper to taste. Add the lemon juice, stirring well. Refrigerate until ready to serve.

❧ Horseradish Sauce ❧

Makes about 3 cups

2 tablespoons vegetable oil
2 onions, thinly sliced
2 tablespoons all-purpose
   flour
2 cups Beef Stock (see
   page 46)
4 tablespoons freshly grated
   horseradish

1 teaspoon lemon juice
1 teaspoon sugar
salt
freshly ground black pepper
¼ cake silken bean curd,
   well mashed

In a medium skillet, heat the vegetable oil over high heat.
Add the onions; lower the heat and sauté until they are
transparent but not browned. Sprinkle the flour over the
onions and mix well. Continue cooking, stirring often, until
the flour is lightly browned.

Remove the skillet from the heat and slowly whisk in the
Beef Stock. Add the grated horseradish, lemon juice, sugar,
and salt and black pepper to taste. Mix well.

Return the skillet to medium heat and cook, stirring
constantly, until the sauce thickens. Remove from the heat
and whisk in the mashed bean curd.

🍗 Ginger Sauce 🍗

Makes 2 cups

S erve this sauce with chicken, fish or vegetables. Ginger sauce will keep for several weeks in the refrigerator in a tightly sealed jar.

1 4-inch piece fresh ginger,
   peeled and diced
6 scallions, cut into 1-inch
   pieces

2 cups vegetable oil
¼ teaspoon sesame oil
salt
freshly ground black pepper

Place the ginger and scallions in a food processor. Process until they are finely chopped. With the machine running, slowly add the vegetable oil, then the sesame oil. Pour the sauce into a bowl and season with salt and black pepper to taste.

🍗 Mustard Sauce 🍗

Makes 2 cups

1 cup sour cream
1 cup Fish Stock (see
   page 48)
2 tablespoons butter

2 tablespoons grainy Dijon
   mustard
salt
freshly ground black pepper

Combine all the ingredients in the top half of a double boiler. Beat gently over the simmering water for 5 minutes or until the sauce thickens; do not let the sauce boil. Serve at once, in a sauceboat.

❧ Hollandaise Sauce ❧

Makes 1 cup

¼ pound unsalted butter
3 egg yolks
2 tablespoons lemon juice

⅛ teaspoon cayenne pepper
salt
freshly ground black pepper

In a small saucepan, melt the butter over low heat.

Place the egg yolks and the lemon juice in a food processor. Process until the yolks are a light yellow color; then, with the machine running, slowly add the hot butter. Pour the mixture into the top half of a double boiler over simmering water. Add the cayenne pepper and salt and black pepper to taste. Keep the sauce warm in the double boiler over very low heat until ready to serve.

❧ Mayonnaise ❧

Makes 3 cups

Mayonnaise, if stored in a tightly sealed container, will keep for a week or more in the refrigerator.

2 egg yolks
2 cups olive oil
3 tablespoons lemon juice

salt
freshly ground black pepper

Place the egg yolks in a food processor. Process for 4 seconds or until the yolks are frothy.

With the machine running, pour in 1 cup of the oil in a very thin steady stream. When the oil has been incorporated, with the machine still running add the lemon juice and then the remaining oil.

Pour the mayonnaise into a bowl. Season to taste with salt and black pepper. If the recipe calls for more lemon juice or other additions, add them now.

Chill well before serving.

❧ Pesto ❧

Makes 2 cups

When serving this classic fresh basil sauce with fish or cold chicken, add the Toasted Farfel. If you wish to freeze the pesto, leave out the Parmesan cheese. Stir it in once the sauce has defrosted.

½ cup freshly grated
   Parmesan cheese
1 cup tightly packed fresh
   basil leaves
¼ cup pine nuts, walnuts or
   unsalted pistachios
2 garlic cloves

3 sprigs arugula or parsley
1 cup olive oil
salt
freshly ground black pepper
½ cup Toasted Farfel,
   optional (see page 217)

Place all the ingredients in a food processor and process until puréed. Pour the pesto into a bowl and add salt and black pepper to taste.

If not using the sauce immediately, refrigerate it in a tightly sealed jar.

❦ Caper-Pickle Sauce ❦

Makes 1 cup

¼ cup wine vinegar
2 tablespoons capers
2 cups white wine
2 sour pickles, chopped

½ cup chopped parsley
1 egg yolk
salt
freshly ground black pepper

In a saucepan, boil the vinegar until it has reduced to about 1½ tablespoons. Add the capers and the white wine and bring it back to a boil. Reduce the heat and simmer until the liquid is reduced by half. Add the chopped pickles and the parsley and remove from the heat.

Beat the egg yolk in a bowl. Slowly add the hot pickle-caper mixture, stirring constantly. Add salt and black pepper to taste.

❦ Green Sauce ❦

Makes 2 cups

1 cup tightly packed fresh
    basil or spinach leaves
¾ cup olive oil
½ cup chopped fresh
    parsley

½ cup chopped watercress
about 3 tablespoons lemon
    juice
salt
freshly ground black pepper

Place all the ingredients in a food processor and process until puréed. Pour into a bowl and add more salt, black pepper and lemon juice to taste if desired. Refrigerate until ready to use.

Desserts

❧ Quiche with Cherries ❧

Serves 6

Pie Crust:
1½ cups all-purpose flour, sifted
11 tablespoons unsalted butter

3 tablespoons sugar
2 eggs

Filling:
1 pound fresh cherries, pitted
8 tablespoons sugar
2 tablespoons brandy

1 cup heavy cream
3 eggs
1 tablespoon cornstarch
¼ cup confectioners' sugar

To make the pie crust, place the flour, 9 tablespoons of the butter, the sugar and eggs in a food processor. Process until the dough clings together. Remove the dough from the bowl and form it into a ball. Dust it with flour and wrap in waxed paper. Chill in the refrigerator for 20 minutes.

With the remaining butter, grease a 9-inch quiche pan; dust it lightly with flour.

Preheat the oven to 375°F.

Cut the ball of dough in two. Wrap one half in plastic and freeze it for later use. On a floured board, roll out the remaining dough into a circle and fit it into the quiche pan; trim the edges and prick the bottom with the tines of a fork.

Bake the shell for 15 minutes or until it is lightly browned. Remove it from the oven and raise the temperature to 400°F.

For the filling, place the cherries in a medium saucepan and add enough boiling water to cover them. Let stand for 5 minutes, then drain well. In a large bowl, mix together the cherries, 3 tablespoons of the sugar and the brandy. Set aside while preparing the filling batter.

244

In a bowl, whisk together the heavy cream, eggs, remaining sugar and the cornstarch. Add the liquid from the cherries and mix well.

Spread the cherries evenly in the quiche shell. Pour the batter over the cherries and bake for 40 minutes or until a cake tester inserted into the center comes out clean.

To serve, sprinkle the quiche with confectioners' sugar and cut it into wedges.

❦ Caramel Pears ❦

Serves 6

1 ounce slivered almonds
1¼ cups sugar
6 tablespoons water
1½ tablespoons lemon juice
6 Anjou or Comice pears

4 tablespoons unsalted butter, cut into small pieces
1 cup Crème Fraîche (see page 231) or sour cream

Preheat the oven to 450°F.

Place the almonds on a baking sheet and toast them in the oven until golden brown. Set aside.

In a heavy saucepan, place the sugar, water and lemon juice. Bring to a boil, reduce the heat and simmer the syrup until it turns a light golden caramel.

Peel, quarter and core the pears. Cut each quarter into 1-inch cubes.

Add the pear cubes to the caramel. Add the butter, stir well, cover the saucepan and simmer for 15 minutes.

Pour the pears and the sauce into a bowl. Sprinkle the almonds on top and cool to room temperature. Serve with Crème Fraîche or sour cream.

Pâte à Choux
with Strawberries

Serves 6

*P*âte à choux is a wonderful pastry dough. First cooked
to a thick consistency on top of the stove, it is then
formed into small mounds and baked. The resulting
puffs are hollow and can be stuffed with any filling you
desire—from whipped cream to chocolate mousse to fresh
fruits or fruit purée. (If you substitute a pinch of salt for the
sugar in the dough and make larger puffs, you can fill them
with sautéed peas or smoked salmon and serve them as hors
d'oeuvres.)

Dough:
1 cup plus 1 tablespoon
water
1 stick unsalted butter, cut
into small pieces, plus
extra butter

1 teaspoon sugar
1 cup plus 1 tablespoon all-
purpose flour
4 eggs

Filling:
8 ounces semisweet
chocolate
¼ cup very strong black
coffee
¼ cup heavy cream

2 pints strawberry ice
cream, softened
1 pint fresh strawberries,
hulled

Preheat the oven to 425°F.

In a heavy saucepan, put the 1 cup of water, the stick of butter and the sugar. Bring to a boil over high heat. Lower the heat and add the cup of flour all at once. With a wooden spoon, beat the mixture until it leaves the sides of the pan and forms a ball. Remove the saucepan from the heat and add 3 of the eggs, one by one, mixing thoroughly after each addition.

Butter a baking sheet. Sprinkle with the 1 tablespoon of flour and shake off any excess.

Fit a pastry bag with a large round nozzle and fill the bag with the dough. Pipe out 16 small puffs the size of a walnut onto the baking sheet.

In a bowl, beat the remaining egg with the 1 tablespoon of water. Brush the puffs with the mixture.

Bake for 20 minutes, or until the puffs are golden brown.

Remove the puffs from the oven. Turn off the oven. With a sharp knife, make a slit in the center of each. Return the puffs to the oven for 15 minutes to dry as the oven cools.

In a double boiler over simmering water, melt the chocolate with the coffee and heavy cream. Keep warm.

Just before serving, fill each puff with some of the strawberry ice cream. Arrange several puffs on each individual serving plate. Spoon some of the hot chocolate sauce over the puffs. Garnish with fresh strawberries and serve.

❦ Sweet Couscous ❦

Serves 6

Couscous is a specialty of North Africa. It is often served with chicken or lamb stew, but I have fond memories of a sweet couscous dish I loved as a child. One of my aunts was from Morocco. For holidays she made this wonderful dish, filled with pistachio nuts, raisins and fresh dates. It is nearly impossible to find real fresh dates, but there are excellent dried dates on the market. In this recipe you can add any dried fruit you have on hand.

1 pound couscous
boiling water
1 pound pitted dried dates
5 ounces candied oranges,
   pineapple, or apricots
4 ounces slivered almonds
4 ounces black currants or
   dark raisins
4 ounces unsalted
   pistachios, shelled

¼ cup sugar
¼ teaspoon cinnamon
2 tablespoons unsalted
   butter or margarine
4 ounces grated semisweet
   chocolate
mint leaves, for garnish

Measure the couscous by cupfuls and pour it into a large bowl. Add the same volume of boiling water, mix well and set aside for 10 minutes.

Line a steamer with a double layer of cheesecloth. Drain the couscous and place it on top of the cheesecloth. Steam, covered, for 15 minutes.

Slice the dates (set aside some slices for garnish) and place them on top of the couscous. Cover and steam for another 15 minutes.

In a bowl, mix together the candied fruit (reserve a few pieces for garnish), almonds, currants or raisins, pistachios, sugar and cinnamon.

248

Put the couscous in a serving bowl. Add the butter and mix well with a fork until the butter is melted. Add the fruit mixture and mix well.

Sprinkle with the reserved date slices, grated chocolate, candied fruits and mint leaves. Serve at room temperature.

❦ Plum Custard ❦

Serves 6

2 tablespoons unsalted
   butter
1½ pounds ripe purple
   plums, halved and pitted
4 eggs
¾ cup sugar
2 tablespoons brandy

2 cups milk
1¼ cups all-purpose flour
1 2-inch piece ginger,
   grated, or 1 teaspoon
   dried ground ginger
1 tablespoon cinnamon
½ cup confectioners' sugar

Preheat the oven to 400°F.

Grease a 1½-quart au gratin dish with the butter. Line the dish with the plums, cut-sides up.

Place the eggs, sugar and brandy in a food processor and process until the eggs are pale yellow. With the machine running, add the milk and then the flour to make a fairly liquid batter. Pour the batter into a large mixing bowl and stir in the grated ginger. Pour the batter over the plums and sprinkle the top with the cinnamon.

Bake for about 45 minutes, or until the custard is set. Remove from the oven and cool.

Just before serving, sprinkle the confectioners' sugar over the top through a fine sieve. Serve at room temperature.

❦ Apricot Meringue Bars ❦

Serves 6

E velyn Gins is my best friend's mother. It is not usual to befriend somebody else's mother, but Evelyn is a dynamic woman, full of life, and above all a wonderful cook. We often have long recipe conversations, where we exchange ideas and solve cooking problems. Evelyn grew up in a kosher home and over the years has developed many nouvelle cuisine kosher recipes. This is one of my favorites.

2 egg yolks
¾ cup sugar
¾ cup vegetable shortening
1½ cups sifted all-purpose
    flour or matzo cake meal

2 cups apricot preserves
2 egg whites
⅛ teaspoon salt
1 cup coarsely chopped
    walnuts

Preheat the oven to 250°F.

Place the egg yolks and ⅓ cup of the sugar in a food processor. Process until the yolks are pale yellow. Add the vegetable shortening and flour and process until the ingredients are thoroughly mixed.

Spread the mixture in an ungreased 13-by-9-inch baking pan. Bake for 15 minutes and remove from the oven. Spread 1 cup of the apricot preserves on top of the cake.

In a mixing bowl, beat the egg whites with the salt until stiff. Gradually beat in the remaining sugar. Carefully fold in the walnuts. Spread the meringue on top of the apricot preserves. Bake for 25 minutes longer.

Remove from the oven and cool in the pan. Top with the remaining apricot preserves. To serve, cut into strips 1 inch wide; cut each strip into several bars.

❧ Orange Liqueur ❧ Mousse

Serves 6

*T*his very quick dessert can be made a couple of hours before dinner. I use an orange-flavored liqueur, but you can use your own favorite liqueur or brandy instead.

6 eggs, separated
1½ cups confectioners'
  sugar
½ cup orange-flavored
  liqueur such as triple sec
  or Cointreau

⅛ teaspoon salt
3½ ounces Crème Fraîche
  (see page 231) or heavy
  cream
6 coffee beans, for garnish

Place the egg yolks and confectioners' sugar in a food processor. Process until the yolks are pale yellow. Pour the mixture into a double boiler and cook over simmering water, stirring constantly, until the mixture is smooth and thick enough to coat a wooden spoon. Do not let it boil. Remove from the heat, add the liqueur, mix well and let cool.

Beat the egg whites in a bowl with the salt until they are firm. Add the Crème Fraîche and mix gently. (If using heavy cream, beat the cream until it is fairly thick before adding it to the egg whites.)

Fold the egg-white mixture into the egg-yolk mixture. Pour into a serving bowl, garnish the top with the coffee beans and refrigerate until firm, about 2 to 3 hours.

Honey Ice Cream with Strawberries

Serves 4

2 pints vanilla ice cream,
  softened
4 tablespoons light honey
1 pint fresh strawberries

4 tablespoons raspberry jelly
1 tablespoon lemon juice
1 kiwi fruit, peeled and
  thinly sliced

Place the ice cream in a stainless steel bowl and mix the honey in with a fork. Return the ice cream to the freezer.

Trim the strawberries. Place them in a food processor and process until puréed.

In a small saucepan, gently warm the raspberry jelly over low heat. Add the lemon juice, mix gently and pour into a bowl.

Place a strainer over the bowl containing the jelly. Strain the strawberry purée into the bowl.

Divide the ice cream among 4 individual serving bowls. Pour some of the strawberry sauce over each serving and garnish with the kiwi fruit slices.

Stuffed Prunes

Serves 6

4 cups dry red wine
1 cup sugar
1 pound dried prunes, pitted
½ pound walnut halves

1 pint heavy cream,
  whipped
½ pound candied orange
  slices

In a medium saucepan, bring the wine and sugar to a boil. Add the prunes and turn off the heat. Leave the prunes to soak at room temperature overnight.

Strain the prunes through a sieve placed over a saucepan. Reserve the liquid. Stuff each prune with some walnut halves. Arrange the prunes in a serving bowl, leaving a small circle in the center.

Bring the wine to a boil again and cook until it has reduced by half. Pour the wine over the prunes. Refrigerate for 2 to 3 hours.

Just before serving, place the whipped cream in the center of the bowl. Decorate with slices of candied orange and serve immediately.

North Egremont Baked Apples

Serves 6

1½ cups pecans
½ cup black currants
⅓ cup maple syrup
6 Rome apples, cored
1 cup water
4 Granny Smith apples, peeled, cored and quartered

about ¾ cup sugar
2 tablespoons Calvados or applejack
1 tablespoon lemon juice
12 fresh mint leaves, for garnish

Preheat the oven to 350°F.

Place the pecans, black currants and maple syrup in a food processor. Pulse the machine until the ingredients are coarsely chopped. Fill the cored apples with the mixture. Arrange the apples in a baking dish and add the water. Bake for 40 minutes.

253

Meanwhile, using the finest side of a grater, grate the Granny Smith apples. Add sugar (use extra if the apples are very tart), Calvados and lemon juice.

To serve, place some of the raw applesauce on a dessert plate, top with a warm baked apple and garnish the top of the apple with 2 fresh mint leaves. Serve the apples hot.

Crêpes Filled with Pear Coulis

Serves 4

4 ripe pears
4 tablespoons unsalted butter
4 tablespoons sugar
3 tablespoons brandy
8 Crêpes (see page 30)

2 tablespoons confectioners' sugar
1 pint Crème Fraîche (see page 231) or whipped cream

Peel, halve and core the pears. Dice them.

In a skillet, melt the butter over low heat. Add the pears and cook, stirring with a wooden spoon, for 5 minutes. Sprinkle with the sugar and cook for 2 minutes longer.

Add the brandy. Heat for 30 seconds and then carefully ignite the brandy with a match. When the flames die down, remove the skillet from the heat.

In another skillet, heat a Crêpe for 5 seconds. Place the crêpe on a plate, place a spoonful of the pear mixture near one edge and roll up the crêpe. Sprinkle with some confectioners' sugar. Repeat with the remaining crêpes.

Serve with Crème Fraîche or whipped cream.

❦ Banana Surprise ❦

Serves 8

*T*he cranberries are uncooked and their tartness is counterbalanced by the sweet bananas. It is therefore important to choose ripe bananas for this recipe. Serve the purée with thin, crisp almond cookies. If you have an ice cream maker, you can use this recipe to make Banana Surprise ice cream.

1 12-ounce package fresh
   cranberries
4 ripe bananas
2 tablespoons liquid from
   brandied cherries

8 brandied cherries
fresh mint leaves, for
   garnish

Wash and drain the cranberries. Place them in a food processor with the bananas. Process until the ingredients are puréed.

    Place a fine sieve over a bowl and strain the purée, pressing it through the sieve with a wooden spoon. Add the cherry brandy and mix well. (If you are making ice cream, freeze the mixture before adding the brandy. Just before serving, beat in the brandy with a fork.) Divide the purée among 8 individual serving bowls. Place a brandied cherry in the center of each bowl and garnish with mint leaves.

❦ Fruit au Gratin ❦

Serves 4

This is a quick, easy dessert. Use whatever fruit you have in the house. However, it's best if you have at least two different fruits. Prepare the recipe in an attractive oven-to-table dish.

3 pears, peeled, quartered
  and cored
2 oranges, peeled and thinly
  sliced
1 banana, peeled and sliced
¼ pound slivered almonds
3 egg yolks

1 pint heavy cream
6 tablespoons sugar
1 tablespoon brandy
  (optional)
2 tablespoons confectioners'
  sugar

Arrange the pear quarters in a circle in a round ovenproof dish, leaving some space in between each piece. Place 1 or 2 orange slices between the pear quarters. Arrange the banana slices in the center of the dish. Sprinkle the fruit with the almonds.

Preheat the broiler.

In a bowl, beat together the egg yolks, cream and sugar. Add the brandy and beat again. Pour the mixture over the fruit and broil until golden brown. Sprinkle the confectioners' sugar on top and serve hot.

🍒 Apricot Bread 🍒

Makes 1 loaf

1 cup dried apricots
1 cup sugar
1 egg
2 tablespoons softened
    unsalted butter or
    vegetable shortening
½ cup orange juice
¼ cup water

2 cups all-purpose flour,
    sifted
2 teaspoons baking powder
1 teaspoon salt
¼ teaspoon baking soda
½ cup chopped unsalted
    pistachio nuts

Soak the apricots in enough warm water to cover for 1 hour. Drain and cut the apricots into small pieces.

Place the sugar, egg and butter in a food processor and process until the yolks are pale yellow. Add the orange juice and water and process for 5 seconds.

In a bowl, mix together the flour, baking powder, salt and baking soda. Add the pistachios and apricots and mix well. Pour the egg mixture into the flour-and-apricot. Mix with a wire whisk to make a smooth batter.

Pour the batter into a greased 9-by-5-inch loaf pan and let it stand for 20 minutes.

Preheat the oven to 350°F.

Bake for 30 minutes, or until a skewer inserted into the center comes out clean. Unmold the bread onto a wire rack and let it cool before slicing.

❦ Cranberry Bread ❦

Makes 1 loaf

F ruit breads are delicious toasted for breakfast, at teatime or served with ice cream or fruit salad.

2 cups sifted all-purpose
    flour
1 cup sugar
1½ teaspoons baking
    powder
1 teaspoon salt
3 tablespoons softened
    unsalted butter, cut in
    small pieces

1 egg, beaten
½ cup orange juice
1 teaspoon orange zest
2 cups cranberries
½ cup raisins, soaked in
    ¼ cup brandy

Preheat the oven to 350°F.

In a large mixing bowl, place the flour, sugar, baking powder and salt. Mix well. Add the butter and mix well.

In a small bowl, mix together the egg, orange juice and orange zest. Add to the flour and mix well. Fold in the cranberries and the raisins and brandy.

Grease a 9-by-5-inch loaf pan and pour in the batter. Bake for about 1 hour, or until a skewer inserted into the center comes out clean. Unmold onto a wire rack and let it cool before slicing.

❦ Orange Nut Bread ❦

Makes 1 loaf

W*rapped in plastic wrap and refrigerated, fruit breads will keep well for several days.*

1 large thin-skinned orange
1 cup raisins, soaked in
  ¼ cup brandy
1 cup sugar
1 teaspoon baking soda
2 cups sifted all-purpose
  flour

2½ tablespoons melted
  unsalted butter or
  vegetable shortening
1 teaspoon pure vanilla
  extract
1 egg, beaten
½ cup chopped walnuts

Preheat the oven to 350°F.

Peel the orange. Cut the peel into small pieces and chop them finely in a food processor. Place the chopped peel in a measuring cup and add enough of the raisins and brandy to make 1 cup. Place the mixture in a large mixing bowl.

Squeeze the orange. Pour the juice into a measuring cup and add enough boiling water to make 1 cup. Add the juice to the orange-peel-and-raisin mixture, then add the sugar and baking soda. Mix well and set aside.

In another bowl, place the flour, 2 tablespoons of the melted butter, vanilla extract and egg. Mix well.

Add the flour to the orange-and-raisin mixture and mix well. Fold in the walnuts.

Grease a 9-by-5-inch loaf pan with the remaining ½ tablespoon butter. Pour the batter into the pan and bake for 50 minutes, or until a skewer inserted into the center comes out clean. Unmold the bread onto a wire rack and let it cool before slicing.

Three-Egg Sponge Cake

Makes 1 cake

3 egg yolks
½ cup boiling water
1 teaspoon lemon extract
1 teaspoon almond extract
1½ cups sugar
1½ cups cake flour, sifted

3 egg whites
⅛ teaspoon salt
2 pints passion fruit sherbet, or other tropical fruit sherbet

Preheat the oven to 350°F.

In a mixing bowl, beat the egg yolks until they are pale yellow. Pour in the boiling water, beating constantly. Still beating the batter, add the lemon extract and then the almond extract. Gradually beat in the sugar, then blend in the flour to make a smooth batter. Set aside.

In a bowl, beat the egg whites with the salt until they are firm but not dry. Fold the egg whites into the egg-yolk mixture. Pour the mixture into an ungreased 9-inch angel cake pan. Bake for 1 hour or until a cake tester inserted into the center of the cake comes out clean. Cool in the pan. Serve with the fruit sherbet.

❦ Passover Sponge Cake ❦

Makes 1 cake

1 tablespoon vegetable
   shortening or margarine
8 egg yolks
1½ cups sugar
grated rind of 1 lemon

1 cup matzo meal
8 egg whites
⅛ teaspoon salt
6 fresh mint leaves, for
   garnish

Preheat the oven to 350°F. Grease an 8-inch-square pan with
the shortening. Cut a piece of waxed paper larger than the
pan and use it to line the bottom and sides of the pan.

Place the egg yolks in a food processor. Process for
1 minute or until they are light yellow. With the processor
running, slowly add the sugar. Pour the mixture into a large
bowl. Add the grated lemon rind and the cake meal. Mix
well with a wooden spoon until the batter is smooth.

In a bowl, beat the egg whites with the salt until they are
firm but not dry.

Fold the egg whites into the yolk mixture. Pour into the
pan and bake for 1 hour, or until a cake tester inserted into
the center of the cake comes out clean. Remove the cake
from the oven and turn it upside down on a rack. Lift off the
pan and peel away the waxed paper.

When the cake is cool, place it on a serving platter.
Garnish with the mint leaves and serve.

Evelyn's Pecan Shortbread Cakes

Makes 16 cakes

1 cup unsalted butter, at
room temperature
1 teaspoon vanilla extract
¼ teaspoon salt
1 cup confectioners'
sugar

2 to 2½ cups all-purpose
flour, sifted
1 cup coarsely chopped
pecans

Preheat the oven to 350°F.

Cut the butter into small pieces. In a mixing bowl, cream the butter with a wooden spoon, adding the vanilla extract and the salt. Gradually beat in the sugar and then 2 cups of the flour; mix thoroughly until the batter is smooth and thick, adding up to ½ cup more flour if the batter is too soft. Mix in the pecans.

Using a tablespoon, drop rounded spoonfuls of batter onto an ungreased baking sheet, leaving some space in between. With the bottom of a glass, press down on each ball until the cake is about ¼-inch thick. Bake for about 15 minutes, until golden brown.

Apricots with Strawberries

Serves 4

In France in the summer, the apricots are sweet and golden-orange in color. My mother used to serve them, cut in two, on a bed of strawberry purée with crunchy almond cookies. It used to be my favorite dessert. When I first came to the United States I was appalled at the taste of the fresh apricots. I could not make my favorite dessert; the apricots were usually hard and flavorless. Today much better apricots are available, although they are still not as good as the French ones. I changed the recipe to compensate, adding some good American maple syrup; the result was a delicious new dessert.

1½ pound fresh apricots, halved and pitted
1 pint strawberries, hulled
juice of 2 oranges
zest of 1 lemon, thinly shredded

¼ cup water
4 tablespoons maple syrup
fresh mint leaves, for garnish
½ cup Crème Fraîche (see page 231)

Thinly slice the apricot halves and set them aside.

Set aside 4 strawberries. Place the remaining berries in a food processor and process until they are puréed. Pour the purée into a saucepan; add the orange juice, lemon zest, water and maple syrup. Bring to a boil, reduce the heat and add the apricots. Simmer over low heat, uncovered, for 10 minutes, stirring from time to time. Pour the mixture into 4 large wine glasses and let cool at room temperature.

Just before serving, place a strawberry in the center of each glass. Surround the strawberry with 4 fresh mint leaves and serve with Crème Fraîche on the side.

Pineapple with ❦ Pomegranate and ❦ Persimmon

Serves 8

1 lemon, halved
3 pomegranates
3 ripe persimmons
½ silken bean curd cake
3 tablespoons apricot
    brandy

1 whole pineapple, peeled
    and cored
8 candied violets or 8 strips
    candied orange peel

Rub your hands with the lemon to prevent them from staining when peeling the pomegranates.

Cut the pomegranates in two and remove the seeds over a bowl. Set aside.

Peel the persimmons. Quarter them and remove any seeds.

Place the persimmons, bean curd and apricot brandy in a food processor. Process until the ingredients are puréed. Pour the mixture into a bowl and set aside.

Slice the pineapple into 8 rings. Place a slice on each of 8 individual dessert plates. Fill the pineapple hole with pomegranate seeds. Mix any remaining pomegranate seeds with the persimmon purée. Spoon some of the purée onto the plate next to each pineapple slice. Decorate with the candied violets or candied orange peel.

❧ Raspberries with ❧ Pomegranate

Serves 6

1 lemon, halved
2 ripe pomegranates
2 cups cranberries
1 cup water
½ cup dry white wine
½ cup sugar

2 pints fresh raspberries
1 pint passion fruit sherbet,
  or other tropical fruit
  sherbet
12 small fresh mint leaves,
  for garnish

Rub your hands with the lemon to prevent them from staining when peeling the pomegranates.

Cut the pomegranates in two and remove the seeds over a bowl. Refrigerate.

In a medium saucepan, place the cranberries, water, wine and sugar. Bring to a boil, reduce the heat and simmer for 5 minutes or until the cranberries pop. Remove from the heat and cool.

Add the raspberries and the cranberries with their liquid to the pomegranate seeds; mix gently and refrigerate until ready to serve.

Divide the mixed fruits among 6 bowls. Top each serving with a scoop of sherbet. Garnish with 2 small mint leaves and serve.

❧ Orange Crêpes Layer ❧ Cake

Serves 6

4 eggs
½ cup sugar
½ cup orange juice
6 tablespoons lemon juice
1 tablespoon grated orange
   zest

1 tablespoon grated lemon
   zest
8 tablespoons unsalted
   butter, cut into small
   pieces
16 Crêpes (see page 30)
¼ cup confectioner's sugar

Combine the eggs, sugar, orange juice, lemon juice, orange zest and lemon zest in a food processor. Process until the ingredients are well mixed and pale yellow.

Pour the mixture into a double boiler. Cook over simmering water, stirring with a wooden spoon. When the mixture thickens to a creamy consistency, stir in the butter, piece by piece. Do not let the orange cream boil. When all the butter has been incorporated, remove the cream from the heat.

Preheat the broiler.

Butter an ovenproof plate. Place a crêpe on it, spread it with some of the cream and cover with another crêpe. Repeat until all the cream has been used, ending with a crêpe.

Sprinkle the top of the cake with confectioner's sugar and broil for 5 seconds or until the top is golden brown. Serve hot or cold with whipped cream.

Glossary

Agar-agar   Clear gelatine processed from seaweed and used in much the same way as conventional animal gelatine, although because it melts at a lower temperature and sets at a higher temperature, agar-agar is actually somewhat easier to use. Agar-agar is sold in health-food stores and Oriental groceries in stick and powder form. It must be soaked in water before using.

Bean curd (tofu)   Soft cakes of soy milk curds that are a staple of Oriental cooking. High in protein, low in calories and inexpensive, packaged bean curd is sold in most supermarkets. *See also* Silken bean curd.

Daikon   Giant white Japanese radish, often grated and served as a garnish.

Dashi   All-purpose Japanese stock made from dried bonito flakes and kelp (*konbu*). The ingredients are easily found in any Oriental grocery. Instant dashi powder is also available. Light chicken broth can be substituted in an emergency

for dashi in recipes that contain no dairy products.

Farfel   A matzo product resembling small pieces of broken matzos; it is cooked and served rather like a grain.

Kasha   Roasted buckwheat groats. The grains of kasha can be whole or either coarsely or finely ground. Packaged kasha can be found in any grocery store.

Mâche (corn salad)   Thin stalk with several small, deep-green leaves. Used in salads.

Mirin   Sweet cooking rice wine. *See* Sake.

Nori   Dried sheets of Japanese seaweed with a dark-brown color. The sheets are used to wrap sushi; thin strips are used as an unusual garnish. Store nori in a tightly sealed glass container in a dark place.

Sake   Japanese alcoholic beverage, made from rice and sometimes called rice wine. Often used in cooking.

Sansho pepper   Greenish-brown Japanese spice made from the pod of the sansho tree. It is not a real pepper and does not taste hot. The flavor is zesty and unusual; sansho is available at Oriental groceries.

Shiso leaves   Leafy Japanese plant of the mint family. Fresh shisho leaves are found in Oriental groceries. Fresh basil or spearmint leaves can be substituted if absolutely necessary.

Silken bean curd   A delicate form of bean curd made from undrained soy milk curds. It is available in supermarkets and Oriental groceries.

Soy sauce   Salty brown sauce with a pungent flavor; in its various forms soy sauce is a fundamental flavoring of Oriental cooking. *Light* soy sauce is thin and quite salty (although low-sodium soy sauce is now available). *Dark* soy sauce is darker and heavier; it gives food a rich, dark color.

Star fruit (carambola) Yellow tropical fruit about six inches long with four to six wide, longitudinal ribs. The fruit forms star-shaped slices when cut vertically. There are two types of star fruit: sweet and slightly sour.

Wakame   Brown Japanese seaweed sold in dried form. The leaves, which are high in nutrients but low in calories, are soaked in water and used in soups and salads.

Index

New Kosher Cooking

toasted with eggplant,
220
Cowpeas with Polish
Mushrooms, 201
Cranberry Bread, 258
Cream of Tomato Soup
with Mint, 55
Crème Fraîche, 231
Crêpes, 30
orange layer cake, 266
pear coulis and, 254
smoked salmon and
artichokes hearts and,
31
Crêpes Filled with Pear
Coulis, 254
Crêpes Stuffed with
Smoked Salmon and
Artichoke Hearts, 31
Curried Rice Salad with
Vegetables, 77
Custard, plum, 249

Daikon, 65
"Daisy" Salad of Endive
and Miniature Beets, 75
Dashi, 45
Deep-Fried Basil Leaves, 34
Deep-Fried Flounder with
Horseradish Sauce, 116
Deep-Fried Olives, 33
Deep-Fried Sardines with
Black Olives, 103
Duck,
beets and, 195
braised with mint, 198
red cabbage and, 196
roast with pears, 191

Eggplant,
couscous with, 220
fried eggs and, 89
kasha with, 218
Eggs,
fried with eggplant, 89
omelets, 90–94
poached, 87
poached with red and
green sauce, 88
Eggs with Cream, 86
Endives
beets and, 201
salad, 75
Evelyn's Pecan Shortbread
Cakes, 262

Farfel,
pan stuffing, 215

toasted, 217
Farfel Pan Stuffing, 215
Fennel and Mustard Greens
Soup, 64
Fillet of Sole with Green
Bananas, 100
Filo, cheese, 27
Fish,
bluefish, 121
carp, 119
flounder, 112, 116
haddock, 80
Halibut, 67
herring, 83, 112, 110
mackerel, 42, 113, 117
salmon, 15, 21, 22, 26,
84, 98, 114, 208
sardines, 103
shad roe, 118
sole, 13, 84, 100
soup with vegetables, 66
stock, 48
Swiss chard stuffed
with, 101
terrines of, 13
tile, 103, 109
trout, 107
tuna, 81, 82, 99
Fish Soup with Vegetables,
66
Fish Stock, 48
Flounder,
bean sprouts and, 112
deep-fried with
horseradish sauce, 116
Flounder with Bean
Sprouts, 112
Fresh Pasta with Tomato
Mushroom Sauce, 222
Fresh Summer Pea Soup, 53
Fresh Tagliatelli with
Walnuts, 223
Fresh Uncooked Tomato
Coulis, 236
Fried Cheese, 40
Fried Eggs and Eggplant, 89
Fruit au Gratin, 256

Garlic Butter, 233
Garlic Purée, 212
Garlic Sauce, 234
Gherkin Croutons, 41
Ginger Sauce, 239
Goose, roast with apples,
193
Green Sauce, 242

Haddock salad, 80

Hamburgers à l'Orientale,
129
Herrings,
broiled fresh, 102
potato pie, 110
potato salad, 83
Hollandaise Sauce, 240
Honey Ice Cream with
Strawberries, 252
Horseradish Sauce, 238
Hot Potato Salad with
Herring and Beets, 83

Ice cream, honey with
strawberries, 252
Italian-Style Rice Salad with
Tuna, 81

James's Fried Onion Rings,
213
Japanese-Style Terrine of
Sole, 13

Kasha Soup with Poached
Egg, 60
Kasha with Eggplants, 218
Kate Goldstein's Noodle
Pudding, 224
Knishes, liver, 181
Kohlrabi with bluefish, 121

Lamb,
boned shoulder of, 150
broiled chops with hot
pimentos, 152
marinated broiled
chops, 153
roast shoulder of, 145
spareribs, 144
stew with apples, 147
stew with celery root
and cherries, 148
yakitori with chicken,
148
Lamb Spareribs, 144
Lamb Stew with Apples, 147
Lamb Stew with Celery
Root and Cherries, 148
Lentil and Red Okra Salad,
73
Lentil Soup, 59
Lentils with Sorrel, 205
Liver Knishes, 181
Lucy's Pot Roast, 124

Mache, 82
Mackerel,
baked in wine, 117

270